WHAT
ABOUT THE
RAPTURE?

WHAT ABOUT THE RAPTURE?

A Study of End-Time Teachings

FaithQuestions SERIES

By Denise Stringer

ABINGDON PRESS
NASHVILLE

WHAT ABOUT THE RAPTURE?
A Study of End-Time Teachings

By Denise Stringer

Copyright © 2003 by Abingdon Press

This book is printed on acid-free, elemental chlorine-free paper.

ISBN: 0-687-08631-0

05 06 07 08 09 10 11 12—10 9 8 7 6 5 4 3 2

MANUFACTURED IN THE UNITED STATES OF AMERICA

CONTENTS

INTRODUCTION
END-TIME TEACHINGS

DRAWING WATER IN DESERT PLACES

It was post-holiday season and I was weary; but sabbath had come at last ... a woman's sabbath. After more than a quarter century of service as a spiritual leader, it was time I found a place of retreat and refreshment. Tired of religion, its talk and its symbols, I needed something honest, something quiet, something real. My ancestors in the faith had beaten a path to the desert when they felt the way I did. I knew I had to go there too.

My journey took me from the Pacific coastline through barren mountains toward the vast wilderness southeast of the Sierra Nevada Mountains. I'd been told of springs in the desert there. In the distance I could see tall palms, sturdy and striking amidst an otherwise arid landscape. They flirted with my imagination.

Soon I discovered a museum that guided me into the mysteries of underground streams and the evolutionary adaptations made by desert plants, animals, and native peoples as environmental conditions changed. I learned that the palms drew their life from beneath the surface of things and that desert dwellers collect rainwater and store it in amazingly creative ways. As I walked out into the wilderness of rock and cactus, slowly and carefully ascending a small cavern, altogether alone, I began to put on this deserted place, to wear its character, to listen with my soul. It was touching me with its history and its images. It was speaking to me of dry places and watering holes.

I'd been told that carrying water was women's work among desert people. Remembering a certain Samaritan woman who regularly made her way to a well dug by her ancestor, Jacob, I began to feel a certain kinship with her. She went in the heat of the day, every day, thirsty and worn by life. On one particular day, however, she went away with more than much-needed drinking water. She went away transformed. It was for her as if she had drunk from the Source of Life. She discovered within herself, the Scripture says, something like "a spring of water welling up within her unto eternal life." She was calling me, much as she called her first-century neighbors, to rediscover myself and my vocation in the One who told her everything she ever did (John 4:7-15).

I would need to find a way to adapt, as desert dwellers had before me, to carry water in waterless places, to drink again and differently. On my way home from the Southwest, I visited another museum in Baltimore. I found there a large collection of pottery from native peoples throughout the Americas. One piece captured my attention and has remained a powerful memory. It was a water jar, in the shape of a woman. She carried a smaller water jar on her back and one in her hands. Shaped of clay, she was dry. As a vessel, however, she was capable of bearing the most essential element of life. So am I.

These are desert times for the people I live and work with. Unremitting global crisis, instantly communicated, exhausts us, leaving us spiritually wasted. The frantic pace we keep and the harsh discipline of our scientific worldview leave us like broken pottery shards, burned by circumstance, mere artifacts of a long-vanished faithfulness.

Because I dare to look up and long for refreshing and rebirth in the midst of the scorching realities around me, I spend time alone. I rest and wait in solitary places until new rain falls. I draw from the wells my ancestors dug. At the same time, I know that I must receive fresh infusions of life through the Spirit that was in Jesus so long ago. Only then can I carry life-sustaining hope back to those in my care.

The end-time visions of Daniel and Revelation, of Enoch and the *Sybilline Oracles*, of Tim LaHaye and Chuck Smith all rely on ancient wells of knowing, like that of our ancestor Jacob. They derive from the work of our forebears in the faith, long before Jesus. Like water from Jacob's well, these sources will leave us thirsty again. Shortly after we have satisfied our longings in the drama and promise of these end-time visions, we will face the waiting and feel the dryness of our desert state again.

The spiritual renewal I seek requires the fresh gift of God with us now, the dynamic energy of life beyond definition and rational categories. This presence satisfies all my longings and quiets my need to anticipate the future. It leaves me unafraid and in awe. It rests my soul and makes me well again.

Invisible Source, Water of Life, Rain of the Spirit: Come fill me that others may drink.

Denise Stringer, August 2002

HOW TO USE
WHAT ABOUT THE RAPTURE?
A STUDY OF END-TIME TEACHINGS

WHAT ABOUT THE RAPTURE? A STUDY OF END-TIME TEACHINGS provides a survey of the origins, development, history, and current debate regarding end-time thought in the Christian tradition. It encourages critical thinking and the development of a viable Christian eschatology for the twenty-first century. The book is designed for use in any of three settings: (1) adult Sunday school, (2) weekday adult groups, and (3) intensive study in a retreat setting. It can also provide a meaningful resource for private study.

Sunday School: WHAT ABOUT THE RAPTURE? may be used on Sunday mornings as a short-term, eight-week study. Sunday morning groups generally last 45 to 60 minutes. If your group would like to go into greater depth, you can divide the sessions and do the study for longer than eight weeks. Each session can easily be divided into two parts to create a sixteen-week study.

Weekday Study: If you use WHAT ABOUT THE RAPTURE? in a weekday study, we recommend eight 90-minute sessions. Participants should prepare ahead by reading the content of the session and choosing one activity for reflection and study. A group leader may wish to assign these activities.

Intensive Study: You may wish to use WHAT ABOUT THE RAPTURE? in a more intense study like a weekend retreat. Allow adequate time between sessions for individual preparation and reflection. Be sure to distribute the books at least two weeks in advance. Locate and provide additional media resources and reference materials, such as Bible dictionaries and commentaries, if available. Tell participants to read WHAT ABOUT THE RAPTURE? and the Book of Revelation before the retreat begins. Begin on

Friday with an evening meal followed by gathering time and worship taken from "Gathering" in Chapter 1. Establish a group covenant as described below. Discuss Chapter 1. Cover Chapters 2, 3, 4, and 5 on Saturday. Cover the remaining chapters on Sunday. End the retreat with closing worship on Sunday afternoon.

Leader/Learner Helps

Leader/learner helps are located in boxes near the relevant main text. They include a variety of discussion and reflection activities. **Asterisks** (*) mark the activities most essential for the sessions. Do these first if your group meets for 45 to 60 minutes. Add other activities in longer sessions (60–90 minutes), for groups that meet for longer than eight weeks, or in retreat settings.

The activities meet the needs of a variety of personalities and ways of learning. Some activities are more appropriate for solitary reflection, and others lend themselves to group discussion or group presentation. An interactive and informal environment will foster a dynamic interchange of ideas and demonstrate the value of diverse perspectives.

Many of the discussion and reflection activities invite the learner to **read specific Scriptures or other resources**. While the readings may be done in the group, reading outside of the session will enrich individual learning and group discussion. Group time can then be devoted to worship, presentations, and discussion.

Each session provides activities for **"Gathering"** and **"Closing"** worship. Worship prepares your group to practice discernment as you study together. A worshipful process of learning provides an experience of Christian community reminiscent of disciples seated at the feet of Jesus. You or other participants may wish to bring some "gift" of spiritual significance from the week's reflections to introduce during the gathering time as an act of worship, for instance, a hymn, a passage of Scripture, a journal entry, or a witness to particular enlightenment. If possible, create a worship center by covering a small table with an attractive cloth. Place on the worship center a Bible, a candle in a candleholder, and other objects that might enhance the session study. Light the candle at the gathering worship.

Most of the sessions include a list of further research options in **"For More Information."** You will enrich your learning by choosing to do one or more of the options listed. You may do these either independently or as a group.

An appendix provides **a glossary** and **additional resources** to enrich the group experience. Words in the main text are italicized to indicate that they are defined in the glossary.

The Role of the Group Leader

A group leader facilitates gathering and closing worship, organizes the group for each session, monitors the use of time so that adequate attention is given to all major points of the session, and fosters an atmosphere of mutual respect and Christian caring. The leader should participate fully in the study as both learner and leader. The same person may lead all the sessions, or each session may have a different leader.

A Group Covenant

A Christian study group practices the spiritual discipline of meeting with other Christians to study and discuss the Bible, biblical theology, current issues, or other topics in an atmosphere of worship, mutual respect, and trust. Develop a group covenant that will encourage such an atmosphere. It should include consideration of the group schedule and time frame for meetings, commitment to attendance, expectations for study and prayer at home, mutual prayer support for group members, and a general approach to the study as a spiritual discipline. Agree on the format for the sessions making sure to include worship at each one. Expect to sit together as though all are at the feet of Jesus, seeking the truth and desiring to follow it with heart, soul, mind, and strength. Covenant to encourage honest, thoughtful dialogue in the context of care and respect for those whose thoughts differ from yours.

Resources for Learning

Each participant will need a Bible, a notebook for journaling or note-taking, and a copy of the book WHAT ABOUT THE RAPTURE? Create a library of additional resources that includes a study Bible, Bible dictionaries and commentaries, and a hymnbook or other worship resources from your church. If possible, include a copy of the *Scofield Reference Bible*.

CHAPTER 1
END-TIME TEACHINGS

Thinking in Terms of the End

The Contemporary Context: Why Thinking Christians Must Engage the Popular Fascination With End-Time Teachings

During the years immediately preceding the third millennium and in the wake of the September 11, 2001, attack on the United States, international interest in end-time teachings increased dramatically. A combination of anxiety and religious sentiment has inspired a plethora of popular preaching and writing by religious leaders, as well as speculation and political activism at all levels of society. The spiritual descendants of Abraham in Jewish, Muslim, and Christian

Focus: An introduction to end-time teachings in their contemporary and historic contexts

Gathering

Greet one another. Care for one another by expressing personal and study-related joys and concerns.

Pray for one another. After a time of silence, pray together using the following spiritual exercise:

Remove all papers and books from your lap. Open the palms of your hands; place your hands palms upward on your lap. Quiet yourself and relax your body. Breathe deeply and evenly. Acknowledge that God is with us. We are not alone. Read aloud Colossians 1:27.

Now, breathe the thought: *"Christ in me."* Repeat this thought several times silently. Now, as you inhale on those words, exhale on these words: *"The hope of glory."* Repeat this breath prayer for several moments. Pay attention to any nuances of meaning that might become apparent to you. Offer gratitude to God for any insights you gain from the prayer exercise.

religions have mined the literature of their traditions for indications of what to expect from God at the end of time.

These three major world religions hold in common "an *apocalyptic* worldview." This theology and understanding of history underlies the writing of the *postexilic* Jewish *prophets*, the New Testament, and the Koran. While the influence and interpretation of *apocalyptic* texts have varied over time, the conceptual structure that they provide frames the religious vision of a huge portion of the world's people. Periods of crisis or rapid change have repeatedly featured a resurgence of appeal to *apocalyptic* writings as a guide for interpretation.

> * What end-time phrases and images do you hear or see in the media?

Without adequate background by which to understand the thought world and vocabulary, philosophical and theological orientations, and spirituality of *apocalyptic literature*, however, today's seeker may feel lost in the face of end-time teachings or be vulnerable to the appeal of unreliable interpretations of Scripture. Because of its deliberately encoded style, end-time teaching is open to a wide variety of interpretations. Without some foundation in the origins and purpose of the content, *apocalyptic* prophecies can increase alienation and fear among faithful people, rather than encourage, counsel, and redeem God's people. This study provides the tools for critical and constructive thinking about the close of history and about the religious literature that has informed Christian teaching on this subject over two millennia.

Jesus and End-Time Teachings

The theology and spirituality of Jesus serves as a constant reference point as we approach the wealth of ancient and modern end-time teaching. Jesus was influenced by Pharisaic Judaism, the *Essenes*, and John the Baptist, all of whom embraced standard elements of *apocalyptic* thought. While Jesus was not himself an *apocalyptic prophet* or seer, he assumed the validity of the general outline of salvation history that had come to dominate Jewish religion since 200 B.C. He believed, more-

> Look at a variety of visual images of Jesus of Nazareth. How do these images compare and contrast with the description of Jesus as a man who believed that the end was near and acted with divine urgency?

over, that he and his fellow Jews were living in the last days. His core metaphor for the end time was "the kingdom of God." According to the earliest layers of tradition, his message was simple: "The time is fulfilled, and the kingdom of God has come near; repent, and believe in the good news" (Mark 1:15).

Clearly, Jesus was a *prophet* who believed that the long-awaited reign of God was breaking into history through his ministry. All the promises of God spoken through the earlier *prophets* were now being fulfilled. Jesus' purpose in announcing the coming of God was to warn the people to turn toward God in faith and obedience, seeking forgiveness and reconciliation. Jesus believed that, in so doing, believers would anticipate the redemption that was imminent and experience the *day of the Lord* as a day of rejoicing rather than judgment. Jesus' vision and mission serve as a standard against which all other *apocalyptic* messages can be evaluated. Jesus' prophetic voice still speaks authoritatively, in spite of two thousand years of waiting for the yet-to-be-revealed dimensions of God's reign.

Speaking in the Prophetic Voice Today

The prophetic voice has always been a force of creative power. The Hebrew Scriptures preserve the record of a long history of spokespersons whom God raised up in each generation to call the people back into covenant relationship with *YHWH* and with one another. According to Isaiah 55:11, when God speaks through a *prophet,* God's word "shall not return" to God "empty" but shall accomplish the divine purpose and "succeed in the thing for which I sent it." To the extent that the prophetic voice offers a perception of history from the divine perspective, it serves as a catalyst for hope and spiritual renewal. Without the *prophet's* vision, the spiritual vitality of the faith community fails. It finds itself searching in its archives for direction and purpose. Unfortunately, that seems to be what much of North American

> • How have you experienced the Word of God speaking or acting in recent times? Be specific. How do you know that the message is from God?

> Borrow a copy of Hal Lindsey's *Late Great Planet Earth* or Tim LaHaye's *Left Behind.* Read excerpts. Describe the mood that permeates this literature. What purpose motivates the author? What makes these books popular?

Christianity is doing in these days of frightening violence and rapid, sometimes chaotic, change.

Many conservative evangelical leaders have made themselves intimately familiar with the old *apocalyptic literature,* long neglected by mainline Protestant Christianity. They have emerged from their studies with an arsenal of weapons with which to fight the enemies of Christ and the reconstruction of Christian faith espoused by more liberal scholars, theologians, and religious leaders. They have created a spiritual climate and culture among their followers that mirrors earlier revivals of *apocalyptic* fervor. Their reframing of end-time teachings in terms of current events and contemporary culture, replete with satellite communication, supersonic travel, and unexplained disappearances of thousands of believers *(rapture)*, stirs hope by predicting escape from trouble, judgment against unbelievers, vindication of the minority point of view, and revenge against those who presume to be enlightened or better informed. The vision that commands their attention may, in fact, reflect an ancient Jewish hope out of which arose the message of Jesus.

An Introduction to End-Time Literature

End-time teachings fall under the theological category of *eschatology.* Not all *eschatology* is *apocalyptic.* An *apocalypse* is a revelation regarding either the heavenly domain or the close of history.

Literature that belongs to the genre of *apocalyptic* expresses eschatological concepts in a narrative format. It records something that a *prophet* has seen and experienced by supernatural means, which is not otherwise available to human understanding. The narrative may describe an overview of history, past, present, and future. It may also document a mystical journey into the heavenly realm, guided

Read on Your Own
Compare and contrast Malachi and Daniel by reading the introductions to these books found in a study Bible. Read selected passages from both: Malachi 3:1-7; 4:1-6; Daniel 7 and 12. How do the two authors differ in the way they treat the future judgment and triumph of God?

and interpreted by an angelic being. The seer (the one to whom the revelation is given) envisions a transcendent reality that exists both within and beyond time and space, much of which is yet to be revealed on the stage of history.

Jewish *apocalyptic* theology assumes the traditional monotheism of earlier Jewish thought. It is built on the premise that God exists outside of history and is sufficiently powerful to intervene in and alter the course of history, since God is also the original cause of the order of the universe. It also assumes the justice of God and God's intolerance toward evil. It anticipates that God will punish those who undermine the well-being of creation.

Jewish *apocalyptic* theology presents the passage of time in terms of a continuous history over the course of many generations. Its *prophets* and seers embrace a linear view of history, rejecting their pagan neighbors' concept of time based on natural cycles. In the end, the one true and living God will triumph over and destroy evil.

According to Jewish *apocalyptic* theology, *YHWH* is the master of history. God's saving acts can be documented as historical events. God took the initiative in creation, intervened particularly in the Exodus and at Sinai, and spoke through the *prophets*. God will act yet again to liberate God's people from the forces of evil. That divine *Parousia* will occur in the midst of crisis and bring history to its

On Your Own
Watch local and international news and review your own knowledge of recent history for information on fundamentalist groups that engage in non-violent resistance or violent acts of protest. What religious beliefs motivate these actions? Are any of these beliefs related to a sense of living in the end times?

climax in an ultimate divine Judgment, leading to the vindication of the righteous oppressed. The *apocalyptic prophet* invariably announces the literal and imminent end of the world, including a final cosmic battle.

The period before the Judgment will be a time of cosmic trouble, replete with natural and supernatural disaster. In association with this final conflict between good and evil, the prophet expects that the righteous will be martyred for their beliefs. With the divine triumph will come either the restoration of paradise on earth or a new heaven and a new earth to be ruled by the righteous servants of God. Beyond the final crisis, the *prophet* foresees either a time of supernatural fertility for the earth or some other form of paradise (*apokastasis*).

A number of characteristic motifs appear consistently in Jewish *apocalyptic* writing. Apocalyptic material uses encoded language and imagery, including animals signifying rulers and nations, as a way of communicating cryptically with the initiated. Typically, the author uses a *pseudonym* that renders the writing authoritative and, perhaps, conceals the author's identity for the sake of personal security. The content of the message is presented as a report of revelation received by way of a vision or dream. Angels and demons are present. The *prophet* sees a vision of the deity, typically in a throne room.

On Your Own
Draw a diagram that depicts time as a cycle of natural seasons. Now create a diagram based on the *apocalyptic* timeline of history. Attempt to experience both perspectives on reality. How might conversion to a linear view of history from a nature-based worldview affect your sense of purpose and understanding of the future?

The interpretation of the revelation is based on the assumption that all history is predetermined in a parallel and invisible domain in which *YHWH* reigns. The prophet perceives history as divided into distinct periods or eras, each defined by a critical event in which *YHWH* intervenes. The *apocalyptic* seer anticipates the resurrection of the dead at the last day for the purpose of a final judgment in which people will be divided into two categories for judgment and redemption. For the faithful, life beyond death will follow God's righteous judgment. Hell and damnation await the unrighteous.

Some of these features can be found in a variety of sources outside Jewish *apocalyptic literature*. Babylonian, Egyptian, and Greco-Roman writings of the same period used various elements of this developing end-time vocabulary. After the Babylonian Exile and the destruction of the Northern Kingdom, however, during a long period when traditional *prophecy* had ceased, Jewish *prophets* brought these features together as a consistent pattern and literary genre.

Early Sources of Jewish Apocalyptic

Jewish *apocalyptic* writing emerged during the Hellenistic Period, between the fourth century B.C. and the first century A.D. Earlier traces of *apocalyptic* motifs and thought patterns, however, can be found in artifacts from other Semitic cultures of the Near East, including the Akkadian and Ugaritic civilizations, dating from two thousand B.C. Other sources of Jewish *apocalyptic* material include the great Hebrew *prophets* and wisdom writers, Babylonian dream interpretation, ancient Canaanite and Zoroastrian *myths*, and Greek and Persian traditions.[1] Exiled Jews living in Babylon were exposed to and influenced by the religion of their neighbors. They used the resources at hand to find meaning in the midst of crisis.

Zoroastrianism, popular in Persia (contemporary Iran) at the time, offered an explanation of evil and of its origins. It predicted divine judgment against evil, called for punishment of its perpetrators. perpetrators. and also offered the hope of a *general resurrection* of the dead at the close of history. The Persian seers understood the universe as being composed of two categories of reality, light and darkness, both of which God created. This conceptualization laid the foundation for the pervasive *dualism* that is characteristic of *apocalyptic* thought. Jewish exiles found this Persian worldview both helpful and compatible with their own thought (Genesis 6:1-4; Isaiah 24:21-23).

The use of animals to represent nation states and rulers was widespread in Greek, Roman, and Near Eastern mythology and became a regular feature of Jewish *apocalyptic prophecy.* While the concept of divine intervention in history was thoroughly Jewish, evidence of the expectation of a cataclysmic conflict can be found in several of the foreign source traditions as well.

Jewish *apocalyptic* represents an original Jewish contribution to world religion, though it borrows from a variety of cultures and religions. It was new as of approximately 300 B.C. It flourished between 200 B.C. and A.D. 100. Christian *apocalyptic prophets* built on Jewish foundations and re-presented the Jewish message in the name of the Christ.

On Your Own

Talk with someone who is fascinated with end-time teachings. Try to learn what attracts him or her to this set of ideas.

The Forging of a New Jewish Worldview

At the beginning of the fourth century B.C., the pressures of the Diadochan wars and, later, the persecution of Jews under Antiochus IV Epiphanes forged this new form of *prophecy*. Helge Kvanig reports, "Here the Jews faced a heathen empire occupying Palestine with formidable religious, cultural and political strength."[2] Its first visionaries articulated a widespread sentiment that the world was out of order and that God was not, after all, in charge. Satan ruled the earth.

The occupying heathens represented a demonic rule on earth that would ultimately be overthrown by the rule of God already being asserted in the heavenly realm. Kvanvig continues, "Thus the apocalyptical universe emerged in a moment when evil was experienced as a power transgressing human limits. It was the experience of non-human evil. The *mythical* and visionary traditions taken over from the Babylonian *diaspora* gave the apocalyptical scribes the opportunity to create a religious universe where these frightening non-human experiences could be included. As a result, a new kind of hope rose in Jewish society, by which the transcendental impact of evil was confronted with a transcendental power of justice. . . . [T]his hope was represented by the sage, Enoch, living in the transcendental realm of God, and pronouncing judgement over the demonic forces. In the Danielic traditions this hope attached to the Son of Man, the transcendental ideal king, who through his ascension from the realm of death would be a sign of liberation for the faithful struggling in the throes of martyrdom"[3] (italics added). The *apocalyptic worldview* allowed Jews to preserve their faith that *YHWH* remained the *sovereign* Lord of history by projecting historic events onto a cosmic screen and anticipating a divinely orchestrated end-time drama on the stage of history.

> **On Your Own**
> Arrange to visit an evangelical Protestant worship service led by a fundamentalist preacher. Listen for themes and messages as they may or may not relate to end-time concerns. Note the hymns selected and the anthems sung, as well as the Scriptures and message. What is the primary vision and motivating hope of this faith community?

Jewish *apocalyptic* writers used *mythic* categories and vocabulary to express deeply held convictions, profound emotions, a stance toward life, and the very nature of reality. Each *apocalyptic* writer felt it to be his duty as a seer, scribe, and spiritual guide to know the work of his predecessors intimately and to reinterpret it for the current generation of God's people. For this reason, a consistent literature emerged out of the earliest *apocalyptic* impulses and images. Frequently, it

> Give some thought to the meaning that you and others around you may take to the Pledge of Allegiance. What other evidence of civil religion can be found in your region? How does it serve as a political tool?

addressed a potential for organizing politically against a common enemy and served as a rallying cry. *Apocalyptic prophecy* empowered a minority population to unite and regroup, in order to resist assimilation and to recover a strong sense of identity and direction.

Notes

1. John J. Collins, editor, *The Encyclopedia of Apocalypticism, Volume I*; New York: Continuum, 1998; page 146.
2. Helge S. Kvanig, *Roots of Apocalyptic;* Neukirchener Verlag, 1988; page 612.
3. Kvanvig, page 613.

Closing
Create a responsive reading by assigning different members of the group the following passages to read aloud: Isaiah 9:2; Isaiah 59:9-10; Psalm 139:11-12; Daniel 2:20; 1 John 1:5. Give all group members a slip of paper on which is written the response: *You are the light of the world; be light in our darkness, O Christ.* You may number the readings or simply move from one reader to the next, based on your seating arrangement. Between readings, let the group take a moment of silence in which to digest the meaning of the Scripture passage before reading the response in unison.

Exchange signs of peace, saying:

The peace of the Lord be with you.
And also with you.

For More Information

Using a study Bible, examine the table of contents and identify the books of *prophecy*. Now turn to the introductions to several of these books to identify the date of each *prophet's* work. Create a timeline of prophetic books. Be sure to include the Book of Daniel.

Find a timeline (or create one) that indicates the "intertestamental *period*" (300 B.C. to A.D. 50) during which *apocalyptic prophecy* flourished and replaced traditional *prophecy*. Refer to a Bible dictionary for help.

Use an encyclopedia to learn more about *Zoroastrianism*.

CHAPTER 2
END-TIME TEACHINGS

Hebrew Sources: Apocalyptic Thought and Literature Before Jesus

Jewish Apocalyptic: Its Beginnings Before the Exile

Although Jewish *apocalyptic* was a relatively late development in Jewish literature, seeds of the thought world were sown long before the Babylonian Exile. While many religious leaders anticipated the *day of the Lord* as a time of elevated significance and well-being for the chosen nation, Amos, like the other great *prophets* of his time, expected something shockingly different. Amos, writing during the peaceful and expansionary rule of Jeroboam II (786–746 B.C.), believed that Israel had developed a fatal dependency on military and economic might. He wrote,

> **Focus:** Canonical Jewish pre-apoclyptic and apocalyptic prophecy

> Alas for you who desire the day of the LORD!
>   Why do you want the day of the LORD?
> It is darkness, not light.
>   . . . and gloom with no brightness in it.

(Amos 5:18-20)

Amos believed that Israel was falsely secure and self-satisfied. God's own people would become the object of divine judgment.

The same *prophet* later saw a vision of summer fruit and interpreted his vision as a warning that the nation was ripe for judgment. He wrote, " 'The end has come upon my people Israel; / I will never again pass them by. / The songs of the temple shall become wailings in that day,' says the Lord GOD; / 'the dead bodies shall be many, / cast out in every place. Be silent!' " (Amos 8:2-3). God had indicted Israel and its destruction was near.

Gathering

Greet one another and share one another's joys and concerns, both personal and those related to this study. Pray for one another, remembering that you sit together as if at the feet of Jesus. Conclude your time of prayer with the following "Prayer for Illumination":

We gather as disciples, students of Jesus, listening for the voice of God and eager to follow. Spirit of God, open our minds to understand, our hearts to receive, and our wills to act according to the promises of God. We pray in Jesus' name. Amen.

Like Amos, Isaiah (742–710 B.C.) envisioned a day of wrath that would force the idolatrous Israelites into caves in the face of divine aggression (Isaiah 2:6-22). He wrote as if he were an *apocalyptic* seer,

See the day of the LORD comes,
  cruel, with wrath and fierce anger,
to make the earth a desolation,
  and to destroy its sinners from it.
For the stars of the heavens and their
    constellations
  will not give their light;
the sun will be dark at its rising,
  and the moon will not shed its light.
I will punish the world for its evil,
  and the wicked for their iniquity; . . .
Therefore I will make the heavens
    tremble,
  and the earth will be shaken out of its
    place,
at the wrath of the LORD of hosts
  in the day of his fierce anger.
(Isaiah 13:9-11, 13)

YHWH would not tolerate forever the rebelliousness and faithlessness of Israel. The Lord would soon display a righteous anger. The "wrath of God" would change the course of history. In the act of destroying the nation, God would prove God's standard of justice and holiness. The Day of Judgment would be the ultimate cosmic event.

This theology served to justify the abhorrence that the *prophet* felt in condemning the hypocrisy and faithlessness of the people. Thus, the violence that the *prophet* prophesied lay beyond moral criticism. Its tragic consequences for his people could not elicit the *prophet's* sym-

Search the news media for examples of ultimate judgments being made today, such as events related to the death penalty or military intervention. Observe nonverbal clues to people's feelings around these issues. Where do you see clear boundaries between human sympathy and justice?

24

pathy. The unfaithful nation would get what it deserved and God's honor would be preserved.

Jewish Apocalyptic Develops During the Babylonian Exile

The Babylonian king Nebuchadnezzar conquered Jerusalem in 597 B.C. He ordered the educated and skilled citizens to be deported to Babylon, lest a rebellion occur. The Temple was destroyed in 586 B.C. Thus began the Babylonian Period, 597–539 B.C.

The exile of Jews to Babylon introduced them both to utter humiliation and to the religious thought world of their neighbors. While *syncretism* threatened the integrity of the faith of the patriarchs, it also offered a new vocabulary by which to work out emerging theological problems. The primary concern seems to have been the sovereignty of *YHWH* in the wake of the long and debasing exile of God's people from their homeland.

The underlying premise of the *apocalyptic* schools of prophetic thought was that the *sovereign* of the universe permits the present evil but will overthrow it in due time. Zoroastrianism held that the highest of the gods would one day step in to eradicate evil in all its forms from the face of the earth, bringing in a new era. The Jewish people began to hope that *YHWH* would return by way of a divine messenger who would preside over an ultimate Judgment Day, much as the Zoroastrians had proposed. The result would be vengeance against the enemies of God's people, followed by universal and lasting peace (Amos 5:18-20; Zephaniah 1:14-18; Isaiah 2:2-4; 11:6-9; Micah 4:1-4; Daniel 7:13). While both the Zoroastrian characterization of evil and its anticipation of a cosmic battle contributed to the formation of an idiom, and Babylonian dream interpretation, astrology, divination, and deification of rulers all influenced Jewish thought and imagination, Jewish *apocalyptic literature* emerged as a consistent genre long after the exiles returned to their own country.

Postexilic Jewish Literature and End-Time Thought

The *prophet* Jeremiah worked between 626 and 587 B.C. Chapters 17 and 25,

> **Read on Your Own**
>   * Read Amos 5:18-20; Zephaniah 1:14-18; Isaiah 2:2-4; 11:6-9; Micah 4:1-4; Daniel 7:13. Note the main ideas. Compare and contrast the various passages. How are the Scriptures similar? different? What, if anything, do they say to you about ultimate judgments? about God?

Read on Your Own
  * Become familiar with Jeremiah 17 and 25, noting any new elements of *apocalyptic* material being introduced. For what purpose does the *prophet* employ end-time images?

  * Read Jeremiah 29:10-14, noting the *prophecy* of restoration. How does this passage speak to you about God today?

both pre-*apocalyptic* passages, come from a larger oracle against Judah and Jerusalem. The *prophet* foresaw disaster for Judah. Babylon would serve as God's instrument in punishing Judah. Ultimately, however, Babylon would be destroyed for having served as an instrument of wanton destruction.

Noteworthy within Jeremiah's plea for vindication (Chapter 17) is his claim that, in spite of the trouble his enemies had caused him, he had not previously desired their destruction or the "fatal day" (Jeremiah. 17:16a). He showed a strong awareness of the dark side of envisioning revenge against one's enemies. Still, his patience is exhausted and he prays that God will bring on them "the day of disaster" (17:18b). The prophet predicted, however, that beyond the destruction lay redemption and the reconstruction of the beloved nation (29:10-14).

Read on Your Own
  * Read Ezekiel 30:3 and 39:1-20. Note the graphic elements of the vision, and compare this *prophecy* with that of Jeremiah. How does the style of the *prophets* differ? Using an art form, such as music or painting, illustrate the contrasting styles of the *prophets* by comparing examples of the work of two artists, for example, Rembrandt and Dali.

Ezekiel took the literature of Jewish *prophecy* several steps closer to what would become the *apocalyptic* genre. He did his work before, during, and after the destruction of Jerusalem and the Exile in 587 B.C. Like the other *prophets* of the period, Ezekiel saw the *day of the Lord* as a "time of doom" (30:3). The political references are coded. The images are apocalyptic. The vast number of corpses, men who lost their lives in battle against God's people, lie strewn on the battlefield. It will take seven months to remove them all (39:1-20). Beyond the destruction, however, comfort and restoration await God's people.

Isaiah 24–27 is also called "The Apocalypse of Isaiah." Technically, it does not qualify as full-blown *apocalyptic* prophecy. It is, rather, transitional eschatological literature that combines the style of the older

26

prophets with several characteristics of what would become the *apocalyptic* genre. It was written between 540 and 425 B.C. This passage offers another oracle of judgment, including a vision of cosmic disruption, earthquakes and other disasters, a harvest of souls, resurrection

> **Read on Your Own**
>   * Read Isaiah 24–27. What new end-time elements does this passage introduce?

of the dead, a heavenly banquet, and final rewards for the righteous. Clearly much of what would become standard in *apocalyptic* literature had already found primitive expression in this passage, which scholars often attribute to a student of the original Isaiah.

Third Isaiah is embedded in the Book of Isaiah, Chapters 56–66. This *post-exilic* prophet's *eschatological* thought can be most readily explored in Chapter 65. It contributes a fresh element to the emerging literature. The author describes a new heaven and a new earth, both of which will appear following the Day of Judgment and the destruction of the earth. Paradise is regained in a new creation.

> **Read on Your Own**
>   * Read Isaiah 65. What does the *prophet* foresee? Compare this passage with Revelation 21:23; 22:1-6; 12, 20. Write a poem or sing a hymn that reflects this hope.

A major concern among those who rebuilt the Temple in Jerusalem after the return of the exiles from Babylon was the preservation of the belief that God reigns in power over the course of history in spite of extensive destruction and the suffering of the chosen people. Psalms 96 and 98 are primary texts for this early vision. These psalms celebrate the ascension of God to the throne as ruler of the universe. Psalm 96:10-13 proclaims,

> Say among the nations, "The LORD is king!
>   The world is firmly established; it shall never
>   be moved.
>   He will judge the people with equity." . . .
> Then shall all the trees of the forest sing for joy
>   before the LORD; for he is coming,
>   for he is coming to judge the earth.
> He will judge the world with righteousness,
>   and the peoples with his truth.

The psalmist's understanding of God as just and righteous required that, while injustice continues for the present and its perpetrators seem to go unpunished, God will one day prove God's power and fairness by condemning the corrupt and vindicating their victims.

Spiritual followers of the *prophet* Zechariah composed the oracles of judgment and redemption found as Zechariah 9–14. They were collected in the fourth and third centuries B.C., possibly interpreting the conquests of Alexander the Great beginning about 330 B.C. They elaborate on the *eschatological* and messianic themes of the earlier chapters of the larger Hebrew text. They include images of a Prince of Peace and of the Good Shepherd rejected by his sheep but slaughtered for the sake of his flock. Notable is the introduction of a messianic king of the lineage of King David and of a remnant of God's faithful ones into an end-time vision of the restoration of glory for the people of God.

> **Discuss**
> Read Zechariah 14. Imagine God's throne encompassing all of present-day Jerusalem. What social and political implications might this vision suggest to end-time *prophets* today?

The oracle envisions a day when God will be king over all the earth and will be worshiped in the purified city of Jerusalem by people of all nations. Following the consummate battle for its preservation, the primacy of the Holy City is established in poetic language as if the earthly Jerusalem is subsumed by its heavenly equivalent. The entire city is seen as the throne room of God on earth (Zechariah 14).

Joel, probably written from Judah between 400 and 350 B.C. during a period of Persian domination, offers an example of *apocalyptic* expectations nearly full-blown, but not presented in the classic narrative format typical of a slightly later period. Joel 3:9-21 describes the holy war that *apocalyptic* prophets predicted. Clearly, it is not only God and God's heavenly servants who will do battle, but the nations of the world (3:9-10). The site of the battle is Jerusalem and the surrounding territory. The metaphor of harvest time, so common in later *eschatological* teaching, appears in verse 13. The *prophet* describes the cosmic dimensions of the *apocalypse:* "The sun and the moon are darkened, / and the stars withdraw their shining. . . . / the

> **Read on Your Own**
> * Study Joel 3:9-21. What new elements of *apocalyptic* *prophecy* appear in this passage?

28

heavens and the earth shake" (3:15, 16b). Beyond the *apocalypse*, however, lies the eternal city enjoying fertility as no earthly city previously had: "The mountains shall drip sweet wine, / and the hills shall flow with milk" (3:18). The fierce justice of *YHWH* is firmly established as a tenet of *apocalyptic* theology: "I will avenge their blood, and I will not clear

> * Create a summary outline of *apocalyptic* expectations, based on your reading of Hebrew *prophecy*. What sequence of events seems to emerge?

the guilty, / for the LORD dwells in Zion" (3:21).

Apocalyptic Thought During the Hellenistic Period (333–63 B.C.)

The Book of Daniel is the only Jewish *apocalyptic* book included in the Hebrew canon. It was originally written as resistance literature, designed to inspire and empower an oppressed people. The *prophecy* was composed during the persecution of the Jews by Antiochus IV Epiphanes, a Seleucid Hellenistic ruler, 175–164 B.C. The collection begins with traditional stories of faithfulness preserved from the late third or early second century B.C. during the Exile. These are followed by a series of visions that describe more recent history as if it were being revealed in advance to the seer Daniel (*prophecy ex eventu*), interspersed with and followed by visions that predict events that were to occur at the end of history.

Apocalyptic writers and their followers believed that historical events predetermined by actions taken in the heavens by God and by angelic beings who represented the nations of the world. According to Daniel's visions, the future held great *tribulation*, particularly in the form of invasions by warring armies and imperialistic rulers, desolation of the Temple, and demise of the Jewish religious life. All of this had, in fact, already occurred by the time the author recorded the *prophecy*. (Note: This is a prime example of *prophecy ex eventu*.) The *tribulation* would be followed by ultimate victory for the Jews and their dominion over the Gentile nations, pre-figured by the coming of the *Ancient of Days* and the *Son of Man* on the clouds of heaven to assert power

> Recall your earliest image of God. Compare it with your current experience or preferred metaphor for God. What are the differences and what significance do they have for faith and understanding?

29

Read on Your Own
  * Read Daniel 7. Compare verses 13-14, using a New International Version of the Bible and a New Revised Standard Version. Look up the terms *Ancient of Days* and *Son of Man* in a Bible dictionary. How does Daniel's vision of a messianic figure coming on the clouds of heaven relate to people's understanding of Jesus in the first century?

and to judge the nations. Clearly, this *prophecy* was based on the hope and expectation of God's *eschatological* intervention.

Daniel 7 provides imagery that has both articulated a universal belief in the fatherhood of God and offered messianic images that have inspired the religious imagination of every generation since its publication. The origin of the widely held image of God as the *Ancient One*, something like an old man with long white hair, robed in white, and seated on a throne, can be found in Daniel 7:9. This passage portrays the divine Person as powerful and vengeful: "A stream of fire issued / and flowed out from his presence. . . . / The court sat in judgment, / and the books were opened" (7:10). The divine Judge is presented as being attended by more servants than the most powerful of earthly rulers. The book opened in the divine court represents the record of the deeds of men and nations.

Compare and contrast the end-time vision of the reign of "one like a son of man" in Daniel 7:13-14 (NIV) and Jesus' rejection of dominion over the nations of the world in Matthew 4:8-10. Note that both passages assume Satan's power over the nations of the earth. What do these two accounts say to you about dominion and power? about one like a human being? about Jesus? about God?

Beneath the surface of the vision and its images lies a profound hatred for the kings of foreign nations. The visionary has abandoned all hope of their conversion or redemption. They are seen as having risen to power out of chaos and evil. Through them, Satan controls the earth and its kingdoms (7:3; also Matthew 4:8-10). Still, the *prophecy* opposes violent uprising as being of little help. Unfortunately, the voice of the *prophet* was ignored. The bloody and fruitless Maccabean Revolt followed shortly after the prophecies of Daniel were published.

The same vision introduces the figure of the *son of man* (translated "a human being" in the New Revised Standard Version) as coming on the clouds of heaven to rule as universal *sovereign* over the nations of the world. In the New International Version the passage reads: "In my vision at night I looked, and there before me was one like a son of man, coming with the clouds of heaven. He approached the *Ancient of Days* and was led into his presence. He was given authority, glory and *sovereign* power; all peoples, nations and men of every language worshiped him. His dominion is an everlasting dominion that will not pass away, and his kingdom is one that will never be destroyed" (Daniel 7:13-14, NIV). The *Synoptic Gospels* (Matthew, Mark, and Luke), particularly when relying on material derived from the final editions of the *Q* material, present Jesus as making several references to the "one like a son of man" described in Daniel 7:13. Jesus speaks of the figure using Daniel's image as a title for the Messiah, *"Son of Man."* In most cases, the implication is that Jesus understands himself to be the One who is coming as the *Son of Man.* No single chapter of Jewish *apocalyptic* material could be more significant to an examination of end-time teachings in light of Jesus' understanding of *eschatology.*

> Re-read Daniel 7:13-14, and note the contrast between the historic Jesus of Nazareth and the heavenly figure like a son of man or a human being. Read Philippians 2:11 as a parallel vision derived from an early Christian hymn. What happened to so dramatically transform the church's understanding of Jesus?

Daniel 12 introduces the *apocalyptic* expectation of a *general resurrection* of the dead at the end time: "Many of those who sleep in the dust of the earth shall awake, some to everlasting life, and some to shame and everlasting contempt" (12:2). The same passage introduces the *apocalyptic* practice of predicting the precise timing of the consummation of history (12:11-12). Three varying calculations are offered, beyond the original three and a half years provided in verses 6-7. The long history of correcting inaccurate predictions seems to have begun here, immediately upon the first attempt at speculation regarding a date for the close of history. Both Chapters 7 and 12 have contributed enormously to the development of *apocalyptic* thought and literature, as well as popular science fiction and mytho-poetic fantasy throughout the course of the history of art and religion.

Read on Your Own
 * Read Daniel 12 and become familiar with its *apocalyptic* features as they are echoed in Revelation. Where does the *prophet* predict dates for the end of history?

Hebrew Prophecy in a Multicultural World

The Hebrew prophetic movement evolved over time in response to changing conditions and cross-fertilization among cultures. The great *prophets*, particularly Jeremiah, Isaiah, Amos, and Hosea, believed that they heard from God through prayer during which they were given the privilege of overhearing the divine voice in the heavenly throne room. In reporting God's thoughts and translating them into human language, they employed end-time images to emphasize the ultimate consequences of continuing to thwart God's law and trusting in that which cannot save. Later *prophets*, increasingly influenced by Babylonian *mythology* and religion and less influenced by older models of hearing from God and speaking for God to the people, used motifs that would ultimately result in a school of *prophecy* known as *apocalyptic*, in which the voice of God is mediated through angels encountered in visions.

Study the hymns in your current hymnbook, and in several older hymnals, under a heading such as "The Return and Reign of the Lord." Examine the lyrics for metaphors and references to *apocalyptic* material. Consider the role of these images in inspiring and sustaining the hope of your congregation. When are these hymns used? Why are some seldom used on a Sunday morning? Choose a favorite and memorize a stanza or key phrase. Listen for the Word of God as God may be speaking to you through the words of this hymn.

Closing

Create a responsive reading by giving each person a copy of Revelation 21:23 and 22:5.

Assign the following passages to be read aloud followed by silence and the group response: Revelation 21:1-6, 23-24.

Sing stanzas 1 and 4 of "How Great Thou Art."

For More Information

Do the following research activities either during or outside of your group meeting.

• Using a Bible dictionary, study the "wrath of God." Compare it with the character of God revealed in Jesus. How and when did Jesus display a similar righteous indignation? How does Jesus' nonresistance and emphasis on forgiveness suggest an alternative understanding of the divine nature?

Look for art work in an old family Bible or a King James Version Reference Bible (preferably a *Scofield Reference Bible*) that depicts God as an old man seated for judgment. Consider the impact of this vision on the religious imagination. How does such an image of God affect one's relationship with God?

Borrow a copy of the *Q* Gospel from your local library. Read the introduction first and then read the sayings collection looking for *apocalyptic* material, particularly the term *Son of Man* with reference to Jesus (Marcus Borg, *The Lost Gospel Q: The Original Sayings of Jesus,* Berkeley, CA: Seastone, 1996). Did the historical Jesus think of himself as the one who would come on the clouds of heaven, or is this an expression of the faith of the church interpolated into the sayings tradition?

Using a public library, search for work by Hieronymus Bosch or other medieval artists who portrayed end-time imagery. Look for etchings or prints related to Dante's Inferno. Consider the impact of these images on the artists and their audiences. Borrow copies and share them with your study group.

CHAPTER 3
END-TIME TEACHINGS

Later Jewish Eschatology

Noncanonical Jewish Apocalyptic Literature

Focus

A look at Jewish *apocalyptic* thought and litera-ture after Daniel through the end of the first century A.D.

The earliest extant Jewish *apocalyptic* material outside of the Hebrew canon can be found in a collection known as Enoch.

Other Jewish *apocalypses* written in response to the destruction of Jerusalem in A.D. 70 were 4 Ezra, 2 Baruch, the Apocalypse of Abraham, and 3 Baruch. Fourth Ezra is preserved as 2 Esdras, chapters 3–14, in the Apocrypha. Enoch was written between 150 B.C. and the end of the first century

A.D. It takes its name from its seer who iden-tifies himself as the bib-lical character named in Genesis 5:18-24. The *Book of the Watchers* and the *Astronomical Book* (*1 Enoch 72–82*) use a narrative format modeled on much older material named for Enmeduranki, the sev-enth of the kings on the Sumerian king list. Enmeduranki founded

Gathering

Greet one another and share joys and concerns. Tell participants, "Remove any materials from your lap. Sit comfortably and upright with your palms open. Pray for one another spontaneously.

"Sit in silence for a few moments. Breathe evenly. Relax your body. Center yourself before God. Inhale the thought, *'Thy Kingdom come.'* Exhale the thought, *'Thy will be done.'* Repeat this silent breath prayer for three to five minutes. Close your prayer time with the word, 'Amen.' Remain quiet for a few moments. If you care to, share your experience with the others."

an association of Babylonian diviners, clearly forerunners of the 'seer who wrote Enoch.[1] Enoch describes a mystical journey into the heavenly domain, guided by an angelic interpreter. It contributes to *apocalyptic literature* the expectation of an *eschatological* judgment of the dead. Among the many other noncanonical Jewish *apocalyptic* works are *Syriac Baruch,* the

> Arrange to view a videotape of the Judean Wilderness, including Qumran and the Jordan River Valley. If possible, find a view of Megiddo and the valley below it, depicting the area in which apocalypticists believed the final battle of Armageddon would take place.

Apocalypses of Elijah and of *Abraham,* the *Sibylline Oracles,* the *Testament of Moses,* and Essene material found at Qumran among the *Dead Sea Scrolls.*

The Essenes

The *Essenes,* a communal movement with a retreat center in the Judean wilderness near the place where John the Baptist preached, left a significant record of their life and thought (c. 130 B.C. to A.D. 68). They viewed the state of God's people and the conditions of the world as hopeless and utterly dominated by Satan. Apart from divine intervention, they believed, the descendants of Abraham were doomed to destruction. Thus they actively awaited a messiah, basing their expectations on an *apocalyptic* interpretation of Hebrew Scripture.

They prophesied that a change of historical eras would come as the result of a final war between God and Satan, to be fought by the Sons of Light and the Sons of Darkness. This battle, sometimes referred to as "Armageddon," would result in the defeat of Satan and of all those who were impure. Out of the divine victory would come the opportunity for the Sons of Light, the *Essenes,* to rule with God over all nations.

In order to prepare themselves for that battle, they separated themselves from Temple-based religious practices and created their own religious centers in several places throughout Palestine, most notably at Qumran. There they practiced ritual bathing and an ascetic lifestyle.

> What spiritual principle underlies the *apocalyptic* hope, espoused by the *Essenes,* that the purity of a remnant of God's people would hasten the arrival of the end-time coming of the Messiah?

Their daily living and observance of the sabbath included common meals and hospitality in anticipation of a messianic banquet and the imminent reign of God on earth. They taught that the spiritual and moral purity of the brothers within the community would hasten the time of the end.

In preparation for the Great War, in which they expected the destruction of the Temple, they copied the Hebrew Scriptures, as well as their community rule, onto scrolls that they expected to use to interpret God's justice. They stored these scrolls in clay jars within the dry caves of the desert near Qumran. In this way, the *Essenes* preserved a body of literature known as the *Dead Sea Scrolls* that contributes significantly to the contemporary study of Hebrew Scripture and *eschatology*.

Early First-Century Palestine: John the Baptist

John the Baptist probably associated with the *Essenes* or was well acquainted with them while engaged in an end-time ministry not far from Qumran. Like the *Essenes*, he was a separatist and an ascetic. He lived a more radically simple lifestyle, however, than did his communitarian neighbors, inasmuch as he spent much time alone deriving his food and shelter from the wilderness. He lived, and later preached, near Jericho, awaiting the Messiah and calling others to prepare for the *day of the Lord*.

> * Read Mark 1:4-8. Compare 2 Kings 1:8 and Zechariah 13:4 with the description of John the Baptist. Study the meaning of the terms *separatist* and *ascetic*. What spiritual motivations and understandings of God lay behind John's self-imposed lifestyle? Why did John choose to live alone in the wilderness? Identify contemporary parallels to this expression of faith. Comparing the impact of John the Baptist and his modern counterparts with the effectiveness of mainstream Christian practices, what advantages and disadvantages do you see in both?

John believed that the coming of the Lord would bring destruction for those who were unprepared and who remained in sin. He understood sin as unfaithfulness to God, which was manifest in corrupt behavior. Thus, he called people of all parties and classes to reorient their lives toward God, to return to just and honest practices, and to acknowledge their prior sin by washing themselves in the water of the Jordan River. This ritual bath would indicate not only their repentance but God's forgiveness. They would be prepared for the soon coming Judgment and would thereby escape condemnation.

John gathered a following, many of whom remained with him even after he deferred to Jesus. They recognized in him a great *prophet* strangely like Elijah. Elijah had been taken up into heaven from beyond the Jordan, near the place where John baptized, after having crossed over the river with Elisha. Popular *prophecy* anticipated the return of Elijah, at the close of history, to prepare the way for the coming of the Messiah. Disciples of John, well after his death, interpreted John's ministry as fulfilling the ministry of the elusive and powerful *prophet*, Elijah. They understood themselves to be living on the divinely appointed stage, themselves playing a part in the drama of the end time.

The Worldview and Politics of Jewish Sects and Parties at the Time of Jesus

According to Josephus, a Jewish historian writing in the late first century, the *apocalyptic prophecy* of Daniel was popular and influential in Palestine during the period immediately preceding the destruction of Jerusalem (*Antiquities* 10:268). Undoubtedly, *apocalyptic* thought dominated the worldview of most Jews from 300 B.C. through A.D. 200. No Jew could escape its impact. In fact, its outline of the historical future, including increasing conflict, persecution of the faithful, and cosmic disruption, all preceding a Day of Judgment, followed by an endless reign over the world by a preeminent and purified Israel was assumed, though the finer details of *apocalyptic* were disputed by some groups.

> Create a timeline of *apocalyptic* expectations. Attempt to create a similar chart of what twenty-first century, scientifically educated citizens generally expect of the future. What similarities and differences do you notice?

The Pharisees

The dominant Jewish party in Palestine, apart from the Temple precinct itself, was a conservative religious and political group called the Pharisees. They opposed the incorporation of Greek and Roman culture into the lifestyle of the Holy City and its surrounding regions, as illus-

> Identify the two distinctive *apocalyptic* expectations that distinguished the Pharisees from their first-century Jewish counterparts. How does the Christian witness to Jesus' bodily resurrection relate to the popular, but much disputed, expectation of an end-time resurrection of the dead?

trated by the pagan *mythology* and eroticism of the theater. The Pharisees, like virtually all Jews of that period, looked for divine intervention to release them from oppression. Anticipating the final judgment, they looked forward to a general bodily resurrection at the coming of the Lord and expected that the faithful would rise from their graves to be rewarded for their deeds. They prayed for the restoration of paradise on the face of the earth and anticipated Jerusalem's serving as the center of a new civilization under the authority of *YHWH* or his Messiah.

Jesus of Nazareth

Jesus looked to John the Baptist as to a mentor during the years prior to his public ministry. It seems that Jesus also associated with the

> Read Mark 14:1-2. Why did the chief priests and scribes fear that a riot would occur? What political consequences might have resulted from a popular uprising at the time of Passover?

Essenes, both in the Galilee and in Judea. The *Essenes* traveled and lived in a number of places where Jesus himself lived and taught as an itinerant *prophet*. They held in common a similar evaluation of the dominant Jewish parties, the Sadducees and the Pharisees, as well as the expectation that the Temple system would soon reap divine condemnation, apart from widespread and immediate reform.

Their concerns and perspective on the practices of faith in the service of *YHWH* emerged out of a similar discontent with things as they were and an expectation that the end of an era was at hand.

> What concerned Jesus most about the religious motivations and expectations of his fellow Jews?

Jesus gathered twelve disciples, an act that some say represents the twelve tribes of Israel, who would rule over the nations in the new age, the kingdom of God (Matthew 19:28; 20:23; Luke 22:28-30). He anticipated the end of the present age within the generation to which he addressed himself. His deepest concern, however, seems to have been that the Jews would rise up against their oppressors, forgetting that God alone could establish God's reign. Jesus anticipated that the Jews would foment a revolution that would lead to the destruction of Jerusalem, rather than to a renewal of the covenant relationship with God, which would bring in the reign of God among them (Matthew 23:37–24:4 and parallels; also, Jeremiah 31:31-34).

The Zealots

Although little written evidence documents the existence of a third Jewish party of Zealots, most scholars assume the existence of an organized movement determined to overthrow Roman occupation. Fears of riots in Jerusalem during the festival of Passover at the time of Jesus, as well as records of various rebellions that took place under the leadership of messianic figures both before and after Jesus' death suggest the persistence of a long-standing armed movement intent on re-establishing the political independence of Israel. This popular resistance derived its vision and doctrine from *apocalyptic* religious beliefs. Passionate hatred of

> Read Acts 1:6-11, 2:43-47, and 4:32-35 for a description of the lifestyle and practices of early Christians living in Jerusalem before A.D. 70. How might the destruction of Jerusalem have affected their expectations for the return of the Lord?

Rome, derived from the economic and political oppression that were daily realities for Jews in first-century Palestine, fueled the volatility.

The Jewish revolt of A.D. 70 led not to liberation and independence but to the destruction of the Temple and the dispersion of both Jews and Christians throughout the Empire. Jesus' worst fears were realized. Those events so shattered the worldview and faith practices of both Jewish and Christian communities that their belief systems and practices were forever altered.

Jesus and the End Time: A Jewish Apocalyptic Prophet With a Fresh Vision

After Jesus came to understand his calling, he returned from both a sojourn in the desert with John the Baptist and a season of solitude to live

Compare and contrast the strategies of separatists and reformers. Explore the beliefs and effectiveness of contemporary Christian movements that attempt to practice their faith by withdrawing from the world. Compare their approach with that of groups like Sojourners Fellowship in Washington, DC, or another intentional community that focuses its evangelistic efforts on social justice work. Compare these approaches with that of the Salvation Army, which does *evangelism* on the streets among the most destitute. Which approach do you think most closely parallels the ministry of Jesus of Nazareth? Why?

and work among the people of the land. Jesus was not a separatist but a reformer. Much more hopeful than his more radically *apocalyptic* mentors, Jesus focused his energy on ministering among those persons who experienced themselves excluded by Pharisaic Judaism. Unlike the *Essenes* and John the Baptist, who predicted divine judgment in the near future, Jesus emphasized and demonstrated the current presence of God among the people to save and help them. While the kingdom of God was yet to be fulfilled, it was already active and available in Jesus' ministry.

The Hebrew Scriptures, especially the prophetic literature, had shaped Jesus' soul and worldview well before he associated with the *Essenes* and John the Baptist. Jesus apparently immersed himself for years in the writings of Daniel, Zechariah, Ezekiel, and Isaiah. He focused on Isaiah 61:1-3 and found his mandate there (see Luke 4:16-20). Jesus understood himself to be anointed by God to announce the inauguration of a new era of divine rule and the defeat of Satan's power. The impact of

the in-breaking reign of God would be consolation and good news for the poor, the oppressed, and those who grieved the corruption of God's people. The long-awaited salvation of God was at hand. It had come near (Mark 1:14-15; Matthew 4:17).

* Read Isaiah 61:1-2 and Isaiah 58:6. Look for evidence in Jesus' actions that he modeled his ministry on these prophecies. What difference did it make to Jesus' message and impact that he identified more closely with these prophecies than with more *apocalyptic* prophecies?

Jesus preferred the term "kingdom of God" when referring to this shift of power, a phrase he borrowed from the synagogue, where

Jews speaking in Aramaic prayed regularly for the coming of the kingdom of God on earth. While the Jews of the synagogue prayed for a future ideal age, Jesus asserted God's authority in the present. God was intervening for the salvation of the world in his own work and words.

> * Examine Mark 1:14-15 and Matthew 4:17. Read them in several translations. Attempt to visualize what Jesus saw as he spoke. How do you see the present and future dimensions of Jesus' core message?

From Jesus' point of view, the *eschaton* had begun and was being realized in every message he preached, every parable he taught, as well as in each healing and exorcism accomplished by the "finger of God" (Luke 11:20). The appearance of this great *day of the Lord* was relatively unremarkable, however, in comparison with the *apocalyptic* expectations of Daniel, for example. Its advent was comparable to the nearly invisible presence of yeast in a lump of dough, but it would dramatically change the world (Luke 13:20-21; also, Luke 13:18-19). God's reign was primarily visible

> Jesus focused on the kingdom of God within history while maintaining a future hope of its fulfillment beyond history. Listen to the prayers and hymns of your local congregation to determine where your faith community places its hope. What difference does it make whether one's faith and hope focus on this life or on life beyond physical death?

through the eyes of faith. According to Luke 17:20-21, "Once Jesus was asked by the Pharisees when the kingdom of God was coming, and he answered, 'The kingdom of God is not coming with things that can be observed; nor will they say, "Look, here it is!" or "There it is!" For, in fact, the kingdom of God is among you.'" The Kingdom was present in and through the ministry of Jesus. God was fulfilling the prophecies of the Hebrew Scriptures.

The kingdom of God belonged, however, to the dependent, the poor, the hungry, and the defamed.

> * Read Joel 2:28-29 and Mark 1:1-8. Compare the *eschatological* message of the *prophets* Joel and John the Baptist with what you know of Jesus' work and the life of the early church. (*See also Luke 12:49-53; Acts 19:1-7.) To what extent is the "baptism" of the Spirit evidence of the fulfillment of end-time hopes?

Compare your discoveries regarding Jesus' authority to teach with your experience of spiritual teaching today. How might our own period be similar to the *intertestamental period* (300 B.C. to A.D. 50) when "no prophet was found in the land"? In what sense is the focus on *apocalyptic prophecy* a substitute for active and original *prophecy*? Refer to 1 Corinthians 14:1-5.

It would ultimately bring a reversal of their condition. It would be their greatest joy and their consummate blessing. Conversely, the wealthy and powerful, who were satisfied with things as they were, would find it very difficult to participate in God's reign. Clearly, Jesus reinterpreted *apocalyptic* expectation and the Kingdom vocabulary of his day, making it a constructive and practical vision of God's salvation active in the midst of the people.

While Jesus proclaimed a current shift of eras and power, he maintained the old *apocalyptic* expectation that what was currently unfolding would lead to a final judgment (Matthew 13:24-30). He reinforced the Jewish image of an end-time harvest of souls, in which the good will be separated from the evil and the righteous from the unrighteous (Mark 4:2-9, 26-29; Matthew 13:24-30; Luke 10:2). The old apocalyptic *dualism* survived, even in the teachings of Jesus, as did the underlying concept of the wrath of God, in his many pronouncements of woes on the scribes and Pharisees (Matthew 23:13, 16, 23, 25, 27, 29). For those who were among the righteous, however, the final judgment would signal the beginning of unparalleled celebration, described in terms of a messianic banquet (Matthew 25:1-13). The *eschaton*, which began in Jesus' itinerant *evangelism*, would soon be brought to consummation.

Using a concordance, read several passages in which Jesus comes into conflict with the Sadducees and Pharisees. See especially Matthew 22:15-46. How did their differences relate to their *eschatology*?

* Read Matthew 19:28; 20:23; Luke 22:28. Begin to draft a timeline of Jesus' *eschatological* expectations. What specific expectations did Jesus have for the future work of God?

For this reason, Jesus addressed questions about the timing and signs of the end. Recent scholarship supports the originality to Jesus of the following sayings in which he discussed the close of history: Mark 8:12; 13:32-37;

Luke 10:17-20; 12:54-56; 17:20; Matthew 16:1-4; 23:29-39 (see also the *Q Apocalypse*; Luke 17:20-37). A careful reading of these passages will result in the conclusion that Jesus expected the end within the lifetimes of those to whom he spoke. The repentance and faith of those who believed his message and received his ministry were the primary evidence he offered for his sense of the imminence of the end. (This was what he referred to when he spoke of the

> * Read and compare Matthew 23:37-39, 24:1-14, and parallels; also Jeremiah 31:31-34. Identify the concerns and expectations of Jesus. Add them to your timeline of Jesus' sense of the future.

"sign of Jonah," Matthew 16:1-4).[2] The opposition that he and his followers faced indicated a dangerous and ultimate choice on the part of his fellow Jews (Luke 9:58; 10:3; 11:23; 14:15-24). Inasmuch as all the *prophets* before him had predicted that conditions would worsen before the final intervention of God, the trouble and corruption that were apparent everywhere, especially in the mounting resist-

> * Read Luke 13:18-19, 20-21. Read these passages a second time for deeper understanding. Take time to visualize what Jesus saw in his mind's eye. Meditate on the images. Compare and contrast them with more typical *apocalyptic* images of the end time. How are they the same? How are they different? Return to your timeline of Jesus' *apocalyptic* expectations. Incorporate this set of insights into your timeline.

ance to Jesus' ministry, provided additional indications of the nearness of the end (Daniel 9:26; 12:1; also 4 Ezra 5:9; 6:4; Jubilees 23:19; Mark 13).

Apart from this, Jesus gave no date, indicated that only God knew the time, and insisted that the consummation of the Kingdom would include a universally recognizable epiphany.

Even though Jesus reinterpreted the popular *apocalyptic* vision, he assumed many of the foundational doctrines of his predecessors and contemporaries. His teaching is correctly described as "apocalyptic eschatology."[3] This assessment simply acknowledges Jesus'

> * Study and compare Mark 8;12; 13:32-37; Luke 10:17-20; 12:54-56; 17:20; Matthew 16:1-4; 23:29-39 (also the *Q Apocalypse*, Luke 17:20-37). What was Jesus' sense of timing for the kingdom of God and the Day of Judgment? Record your insights on your timeline.

> Search several hymnals for hymns that celebrate or pray for the coming of the kingdom of God. Study the theology and consider the biblical references used by the hymn writers. Find one hymn that speaks to you. Meditate on a key phrase or stanza. Consider committing it to memory.

worldview and does not imply that he wrote anything in the *apocalyptic* literary genre or that he reported visions in which angels mediated otherwise unavailable information about either the heavenly realm or the future.

Among the characteristic features of the genre that Jesus incorporated uncritically, however, are the bodily resurrection of the dead for judgment at the close of history (see Luke 11:31-32), the promise of life beyond death (see Mark 9:43-47), and the expectation of the restoration of Israel to preeminence among the nations (Luke 13:28-29; also Matthew 8:11-12). In these ways, he remained closely aligned with the Pharisees whose teachings dominated the synagogues of Galilee where Jesus spent the majority of his life and ministry.

Jesus very probably also assumed the appearance in the clouds of heaven of "one like a son of man," as described in Daniel 7:13. Jesus believed that he and his followers lived in the end times. It was urgent that all Jews repent and believe the good news of his message: "The kingdom of God has come near" (Mark 1:15).

Notes

1. Murphy, Frederick J., "Introduction to Apocalyptic Literature," *New Interpreter's Bible, Vol. VII;* Nashville: Abingdon, 1996; pages 1–5.

2. Robert Jewett, *Jesus Against the Rapture*; Philadelphia: Westminster Press, 1979; page 79.

3. Dale Allison, "The Eschatology of Jesus," *The Encyclopedia of Apocalypticism, Volume I, The Origins of Apocalypticism in Judaism and Christianity,* edited by John J. Collins; New York: Continuum, 1998; page 267.

Closing

Stand in a circle. Extend your arms in front of you until you can look at the palms of your hands. This gesture suggests that you are poised to receive and makes Jesus' announcement that the kingdom of God "is at hand" both vivid and dynamic. Pray the Lord's Prayer in unison, slowly and deliberately, with eyes open and hands extended.

Sing the hymn, "O Day of God Draw Nigh."

Exchange the blessing:
The peace of the Lord be with you.
And also with you.

For More Information

Using an encyclopedia, learn more about the *Dead Sea Scrolls* and the *apocalyptic* thought of the *Essenes*. How is it like that of Jesus? How is it different?

Using a Bible atlas or a contemporary map of Israel, locate Qumran and the place where the Jordan River meets the Dead Sea. Locate Jericho and the place where John the Baptist is believed to have baptized Jesus. Envision this as a meeting place for *prophets*, separatists, and sojourners, as well as pilgrims seeking spiritual renewal in places where the prophets Elijah and Elisha had met with God. What impact might such a setting have on people living there in isolation over long periods?

CHAPTER 4
END-TIME TEACHINGS

The Faith of the Church:
Examining the Historical Evidence

The *Parousia* and the Early Church

> **Focus:** The faith and *eschatology* of the first-century Christian movement

From the earliest days after Jesus' death and resurrection, believers both celebrated his continuing presence and looked forward to his return. While the formal doctrine of the *second coming of Christ* emerged in the late second and third centuries, the editors of the *Q*, or sayings gospel, linked a visible reappearing of the exalted Lord to the expectation of the coming of the Son of Man on the clouds of heaven as early as the fifties A.D. (Matthew 19:28; Luke 22:28-30; Matthew 24:26-28, 37-44; and Luke 12:39-40; 17:23-24, 37; also Matthew 10:23; 13:41; 16:27-28; 26:64; Mark 8:38, 13:26).

The apostle Paul, writing in the same

> **Gathering**
> Greet one another and share one another's joys and concerns. Pray for one another. Remember that you gather as if at the feet of Jesus. Conclude your gathering time with the following prayer for illumination:
>
> *Spirit of God: We acknowledge our dependency upon you for life, for insight, for correction, and for redemption. Open our hearts and minds to hear your life-giving Word as we search the Scriptures and learn together. We study and we pray in the name of Jesus, our Lord. Amen.*
>
> Sing the worship chorus, "Lead Me, Lord."

period, anticipated the presence of Christ at the consummation of history and addressed the pastoral problem posed by the death of believers before the *Parousia* (1 Corinthians 15:20-28; 1 Thessalonians 4:13-18; also 1 Thessalonians 1:9-10). Paul reassured believers that just as Christ rose from the dead and was given an immortal body, so also will those who have

> Locate a copy of the Nicene and Apostles' Creeds in your church's worship resources. Find references to the end times. Consider what the original authors intended by these words. What do you think twenty-first–century Christians mean when they recite these lines of the creeds? Write your own statement of faith regarding the Second Coming and Final Judgment.

died rise to a new life with Christ at his appearing. Only then will those who remain alive at his coming enter the eternal kingdom of the Father. Later first-century New Testament writers clarified the expectation further (see Matthew 23:39; Acts 1:11; John 21:22-23; Hebrews 9:28).

As the first century waned, however, and the generation of Jews who were alive at the time of Jesus' public ministry died, a theological as well as a pastoral problem emerged. Later scholars, reflecting on the spiritual crisis caused by the passage of time, have referred to it as the

> Read 1 Corinthians 15:20-28; 1 Thessalonians 4:13–5:11. Outline Paul's end-time chronology of events

"Delay of the *Parousia*." The pastoral epistle, Second Peter, addressed the problem that had previously surfaced in the churches at Thessalonica and Corinth (2 Peter 3:1-10). The author deals with the delay of the Lord's return by suggesting that God's timing differs from human calculations. Moreover, the delay provides for further evangelistic work and demonstrates God's primary desire to bring all humanity to repentance and to the kingdom of God.

Early Christians conceived of the Lord as coming in the sky above the earth at the close of history. They believed that the faithful would be lifted up to meet him and enjoy communion with him for-

> * Study 1 Thessalonians 4:14-17 and 1 Corinthians 15:50-57. Compare the *prophecy* given "by the word of the Lord" through the apostle Paul with Daniel 7:13-14, 18. Note the additions that Paul makes to Daniel's predictions. (See Luke 17:34, 35; Matthew 24:40-41.)

ever in a new heaven and new earth (1 Thessalonians 4:14, 17; also, 1 Corinthians 15:52; Luke 17:34-35; Matthew 24:40-41). Notice that, contrary to the modern *doctrine of the rapture*, the resurrection of the dead and the rising of those who are alive were understood as events that would occur consecutively in the last moments of history, after much suffering and endurance; rather than as an interim event by which the righteous escape the *tribulation* and death that are to plague the unrighteous.

The Apostle Paul: An Apocalyptic Visionary and Evangelist

Paul had been steeped in Jewish *apocalyptic* from childhood. Having seen the Lord by revelation, he was certain that the Messiah whom the Jews awaited was none other than Jesus, risen from the dead and currently reigning. He believed that Jesus would establish his dominion over all nations, especially through the preaching of the gospel. Ultimately, Jesus would "hand over the kingdom to God the Father, after he has destroyed every ruler and every authority and power. For he must reign until he has put all his enemies under his feet. . . . When all things are subjected to him, then the Son himself will also be subjected to the one who put all things in subjection under him, so that God may be all in all" (1 Corinthians 15:24-28). Paul anticipated a future fulfillment of the Kingdom when he wrote, "We ourselves, who have the first fruits of the Spirit, groan inwardly while we wait for adoption, the redemption of our bodies" (Romans 8:23; also, verse 24).

Mark's Gospel

Of the four canonical Gospels, Mark's Gospel was written first, probably during the war that led to the destruction of Jerusalem and to the dispersion of both Jews and Christians. Mark believed that history was moving toward an *eschatological* re-creation of the original paradise. This new creation would be the fulfillment of God's reign. Clearly, like the *Q* community, Mark saw in Jesus one who would fulfill the vision recorded in Daniel 7.

The constant activity of Jesus in Mark's narrative reflects the pressure that Mark and his readers may well have been feeling while under the persecution of Nero in Rome. According to Mark, Jesus had been urgent about spreading the word swiftly before the *day of the Lord*. So also, time seemed short for the church in mission to the Greco-Roman world. The war in Jerusalem, the "desolating sacrilege" of an image of the emperor now stationed in the Temple (Mark 13:14), and the presence of pretenders who claimed to be the Christ preaching among the Christian communities contributed to an emerging sense that the end was near. The period in which Mark wrote was one of heightened *apocalyptic* thinking.

Matthew's Gospel

Matthew wrote well after the destruction of Jerusalem and after a great deal of thought had been given to the meaning of Jesus' life, death, and resurrection in light of the mission of the church and the delay of his coming. Matthew's Jesus is a key figure in the long journey toward the salvation of God's people and the redemption of humankind. His mission is to be God's representative in the work of defeating evil.

Matthew portrays Jesus as greater than Satan. Jesus' survival of the slaying of the infants in Bethlehem, his wisdom in responding to his enemies and critics, his power over Satan in both exorcisms and healing ministry, his obedience to God unto death, and his resurrection from the dead foreshadow the ultimate defeat of evil that is yet to occur. The author believed the life and ministry of Jesus paved the way that would lead to the triumphant coming of the *Son of Man*. On that day Jesus would judge humankind, cast Satan

> **The Defeat of Satan and Evil**
> Note the emphasis in the *Synoptic Gospels* on Jesus' struggle with Satan and his defeat of Satan in a wide variety of settings. *Apocalyptic* doctrine taught that Satan ruled the nations of the world. God was *sovereign* over the universe but allowed Satan to control the earth temporarily. Jesus came to unsettle Satan's rule and to initiate his defeat. The kingdom of God on earth had begun. Do you view the world as being dominated by evil or under the rule of Christ? Describe your assessment of the work of Christ in defeating evil to date.

> **Jesus as Son of Man**
> Read Matthew 19:28; 24:26-28, 37-44; and Luke 12:39-40; 17:23-24, 30. All of this material comes from *Q*. The majority of recent scholarship suggests that the references to Jesus as the heavenly *Son of Man* represent late additions made by editors. The debate over Jesus' use of the reference from Daniel 7:13-14 continues unresolved.

49

Consider the power and meaning of Matthew's call to the church "to live in anticipation of the victory of God over evil, a victory already won in the hearts and minds of the believers." To what extent is this call already being realized in you and among the believers of your community? Review the history of the church as you know it and wonder about the fruit of Matthew's message over two millennia. Rededicate yourself to God and renew your commitment to resist evil, injustice, and oppression in whatever forms they present themselves.

out of the sphere of history, and establish the reign of God on earth. The writer called the church to live in anticipation of the victory of God over evil, a victory already won in the hearts and minds of the believers.

In Matthew, the Jews have rejected their Messiah and will be excluded from the kingdom of God. The gospel must now be taken to the Gentiles. The delay of the Lord's coming will make it possible for the gospel to be preached and taught throughout the world. In the meantime,

the Lord remains with the church until the Kingdom is fulfilled (Matthew 28:16-20).

* Read the Great Commission from Matthew 28:18-20. Rewrite the instructions of the risen Lord to the church in your own words. Note the significance, in light of the apparent delay of his returning, of his promise, "I am with you always, to the end of the age." Describe the difference in spirituality and mood between the final passage of Matthew's Gospel and that of Mark (see mark 16:8 and Mark 16:19-20).

Luke's Gospel

Like Matthew, Luke wrote after sufficient time had passed to provide for extensive theological reflection on Jesus' ministry and its significance. Luke presented Jesus' life and ministry as the revelation of the way of salvation for the world. Luke believed that Satan ruled the world until Jesus defeated him during the temptations in the wilderness (Luke 4:1-13). The defeat of Satan, however, only began at that point. It continued through healings, exorcisms, and preaching, all of which led to repentance and redemption of lives. Once more Satan attacked Jesus in the betrayal by Judas (Luke 22:3, 47-54a), the arrest, the trial, and the Crucifixion. God raised Jesus from the dead, however, defeating Satan in his attempt to destroy Jesus. Jesus' power over Satan was the result of the outpouring of the Holy Spirit at his baptism, his continuing life of prayer, and his pursuit of God's purpose. Likewise, the power of the disciples over evil, including disease, was the result of their following Jesus' example and of the Spirit's working through them (10:17-19).

When Jesus died, he returned his "spirit" to God (23:46); at Pentecost he poured out his "spirit" upon the church (Acts 2:33). Thus, the church carries on the work of defeating Satan and bringing the reign of God into human history through preaching, teaching, and healing. As God inaugurated history, God also guides the process of history and will bring it to conclusion at some future time (Luke 12:40). While Jesus came first for the Jews, the center of God's work is no longer Jerusalem but Rome. The gospel will be disseminated by the disciples throughout the known world (24:47).

At the end, when the kingdom of God comes in fullness, all humanity will be judged. Those who are saved will be those who are truly repentant and obedient to God's word (13:22-30). At that time the *Son of Man* will be revealed in his heavenly form.

The Little Apocalypses

The so-called "Little Apocalypses" found in the Gospels of Matthew, Mark, and Luke, do not hold up under the scrutiny of rigorous scholarship as being discourses originating with Jesus. They are viewed as anthologies of Jesus' sayings reinterpreted for the church some time after Jesus' death (Mark 13:5-37; Matthew 24:24-36; 25; Luke 21:8-36). Scholars attribute these collections of end-time teachings to Christian teachers and pastors writing between A.D. 70 and the mid-80's. These Christian leaders wanted to discourage heretical *prophecy*, encourage endurance, and reassure believers that the end would come soon. It seems that false messiahs appeared from time to time, offering signs of the end. The apostolic witness declared that no sign would be given other than the truth already revealed in and through Jesus.

> * Read and become familiar with the "Little Apocalypses" found in Mark 13:5-37; Matthew 24:24-36; 25; and Luke 21:8-36. Note the slight differences among them. Create a separate timeline for these *apocalypses*, and compare it with your earlier timeline of Jesus' end-time expectations. What differences can you identify?

The Gospel of John: An Alternative Vision

John's Gospel interpreted the Hebrew concept of the *day of the Lord* in a revisionist manner, largely rejecting the standard *apocalyptic* timeline. The author of the Gospel of John and his readers came under the influence of Neo-Platonism and, given the apparent failure of *apocalyptic* predictions, the author reinterpreted the classic final Judgment as having already occurred in Jesus' crucifixion: "Now is the judgment of this world; now the ruler of this world will be driven out. And I, when I am lifted up from the earth, will draw all people to myself" (John 12:31-32; also, 3:19; 5:22, 27).

The author presented the Lord as having come again in the Resurrection when he imparted the Holy Spirit to the church: "He breathed on them and said to them, 'Receive the Holy Spirit' " (20:22). According to John, Jesus had predicted his return in this way before his crucifixion: "If you love me, you will keep my commandments. And I will ask the Father, and he will give you another Advocate, to be with you forever. . . . In a little while the world will no longer see me, but you will see me. . . . They who have my commandments and keep them are those who love me; and those who love me will be loved by my Father, and I will love them and reveal myself to them. . . . Those who love me will keep my word and my Father will love them, and we will come to them and make our home with them" (14:15-23).

> * Read John 12:31-32; also, 3:19; 5:22, 27; 3:16; and 17:24. Digest the *eschatology* behind these passages. Attempt to diagram it.

The *day of the Lord*, therefore, in John's Gospel, is no longer a cosmic display simultaneously visible to all as the final scene of history, but an invisible imparting of divine wisdom and love in the form of the indwelling Spirit. Thus, "the true worshipers will worship the Father in spirit and in truth" (4:23). The mutuality of Father, Son, and Holy Spirit shall be experienced among the believers in their union with God (see 17:20-24). Still, the believer is to expect a timeless and glorious union with God beyond physical life (3:16; 17:24).

The futuristic focus of *apocalyptic* thought in John's Gospel is largely supplanted by an invitation to participate in the divine life now. The goal is to experience eternal life in the present. Believers can partake of the timeless reality of God in each moment of faithful living.

In John, Jesus' kingdom is apolitical. It no longer connotes a reversal of economic circumstance for the poor, the orphaned, the widow, and those who mourn. It does not threaten existing power structures. The reign of Christ is not the prophetic reign of justice but a

> What is your expectation for the course of history for the foreseeable future? What is your personal *eschatology*?

spiritual reality based in the knowledge of God and a sincere approach to God through faith.

C. H. Dodd, in his important work, *The Interpretation of the Fourth Gospel*,[1] wrote: "Jesus neither accepts explicitly nor rejects the appellation 'king', but in saying, 'My kingdom is not of this world', He admits by implication that He is a king in a non-worldly sense; and this sense is explained in the words 'For this I was born, and for this I came into the world, to bear witness to the Truth. Everyone who belongs to the Truth hears my voice' (xviii. 37). That is to say, the kingship of the Messiah is the sovereignty of the Truth which He reveals and embodies. In virtue of this He demands obedience from men."[2]

John does, however, use the original vocabulary of the kingdom of God in one instance, thus giving evidence of his reliance on the apostolic tradition and his familiarity with the historical message of Jesus: "Very truly, I tell you, no one can see the kingdom of God without being born from above . . . without being born of water and Spirit" (3:3, 5). To participate in the kingdom of God requires a spiritual rebirth. While Jesus preexisted creation and became incarnate by the will of the Father, others must go through a radical and saving transformation: "To all who received him, who believed in his name, he gave power to become children of God, who were born, not of blood or of the will of the flesh or of the will of man, but of God" (1:12-13).

The kingdom of God, from John's point of view, is the state of being in God uniquely manifest within the church. The *dualism* of *apocalyptic* (God versus the devil; good versus evil; the sanctified versus the worldly) has been replaced by a doctrine of two domains: the visible or unreal and the invisible and real. Believers already participate in the invisible domain of the Spirit as they partake of eternal life now. They have already passed through death into life. There is no longer any need for a linear view of history. While the first century remained a largely *apocalyptic* environment for both Jews and Christians, Greek and Roman philosophical categories and social concerns contributed significantly to the evolution of the faith.

Closing

Using the baptism ritual in your church's worship resources, remember your baptism and reaffirm your faith.

Sing the hymn, "Go Make of All Disciples," or another favorite hymn about the call to make disciples. Look for one in your church's hymnbook.

Offer one another signs of peace with the words:

The peace of the Lord be with you.
And also with you.

Notes

1. Cambridge University Press, 1953.

2. Ibid., page 229.

For More Information

Using an encyclopedia, learn more about the reign of the emperor Nero and the conditions of the Roman Empire under his rule. Explore the impact of his power on Christians living in Jerusalem and in Rome. What relationship might exist between the burning of Rome in A.D. 64 and the images of *apocalypse* found in Mark 13?

Using an encyclopedia, learn about "neo-Platonism." Look for indications of its *eschatology*.

Using your local library, learn what you can about early Christian *"gnosticism."* John's Gospel addressed this unorthodox expression of Christianity insisting that Jesus was truly a man, actually died, and was literally and physically raised from the dead. He insisted, moreover, that the knowledge of God was available through Christ to anyone who believed in him, rather than to a select group of initiates. Moreover, he declared that this faith brought eternal life. Consider how, in spite of John's debate with *Gnosticism*, his *eschatology* may reflect Gnostic categories.

CHAPTER 5
END-TIME TEACHINGS

Revelation and Other Late First-Century Christian Apocalyptic Literature

Christian writers adapted Jewish *apocalyptic* outlines and stylistic elements to the Christian message in an attempt to instruct the faithful regarding the future dimensions of the kingdom of God. They

> **Focus**
> The Book of Revelation and its interpretation

sought to encourage the church's endurance in the midst of persecution and social upheaval. Just as the apostle Paul, for example, inserted the

---

Gathering
Greet one another using the ancient exchange:
Leader: The Lord be with you.
Response: And also with you.
If you are meeting in the morning, sing, "See the Morning Sun Ascending," or another hymn that draws on the Book of Revelation as its scriptural basis. Consider also stanzas 1, 3, and 4 of "Let All Mortal Flesh Keep Silence." Observe a time of silent meditation during which you ponder the greeting and the hymn you have just shared.

Express your joys and concerns, and pray for one another. Read Charles Wesley's hymn "Whether the Word Be Preached or Read," or pray the following prayer from Kenya, "For the Spirit of Truth":

From the cowardice that dares not face new truth,
from the laziness that is contented with half-truth,
from the arrogance that thinks it knows all truth,
Good Lord, deliver me. Amen.

---

return of Christ where Daniel and the *Q* community envisioned the appearing of one like a *Son of Man,* so later authors, both canonical and noncanonical, adapted the old rubric to a new faith. As Paul interpolated the doctrine of justification by grace through faith into the Jewish vision of a just God executing judgment, so later Christian teachers inserted Christian themes into the old *apocalyptic* outline of the future. In doing so, they drew upon the Spirit of Christ for fresh wisdom in the midst of changing pastoral needs and the increasingly Gentile context for mission (Romans 3:21–4:25; 9:30–10:13; Philippians 3:2-11).

What remained intact, however, was the old *apocalyptic* concept of *universal history.* Like the Jewish *prophets* before them, the Christian futurists expected God to direct a future that would have an impact on all of creation. They anticipated ever-increasing trouble worldwide, especially in the form of religious persecution. It would be followed by divine intervention, judgment against the enemies of God's people, and the vindication of the righteous. After the judgment would come a restoration of the original paradise, either on earth or in a heavenly dimension. God's vice-regent would oversee the universal peace under God's *sovereign* dominion (1 Corinthians 15:22-28; also, Daniel 9:26; 4 Ezra 5:9; 6:4; Jubilee 23:19).

> Read Romans 3:21–4:25; 9:30–10:13; Philippians 3:2-14. Compare the *apocalyptic* notion of being caught up to be with the Lord at his coming and the doctrine of justification by grace through faith that assures the believer of escaping condemnation, having already been acquitted by faith based on the witness of Jesus' life, death, and resurrection. Read 1 Thessalonians 1:9-10. How are the two concepts different perspectives on the same reality? (See also Romans 2:1-11; 14:10-12.)

The Revelation to John, more than any other New Testament literature, focuses attention on the end times, detailing them in light of contemporary history and yet to be realized expectations. Revelation was built on the Jewish *apocalyptic* foundations that had been laid at least three hundred years earlier.

Revelation

Revelation continues to be the single most influential piece of Christian end-time teaching. Its perennial influence on faithful people commands respect and should be understood. Taking the text of Revelation seriously requires careful study of the book's character and distinctive doctrines in light of the teachings of Jesus and all available tools of critical analysis. Most important, an appropriate reading of Revelation requires deeply faithful listening.

> * What is the status of your hope for the world's redemption, on a scale of zero to ten, with zero representing no hope, one being very pessimistic, and ten being hopeful? Why? How would you assess the level of Jesus' hopefulness as he instructed his disciples to pray, "Thy kingdom come on earth as it is in heaven"? Pray that one line of the Lord's Prayer now, and make a habit of doing it regularly.

The Book of Revelation is the only example of pure *apocalyptic literature* in the New Testament canon. It is of the same genre as the Book of Daniel and builds on the prophecies of Ezekiel and Enoch. In fact, of 404 verses, 275 include allusions to Old Testament Scripture.[1] Some have argued that this text is thoroughly Jewish, both in style and in theology, though the author has made the expected interpolations of the Christ figure and ostensibly records the very words of the risen and exalted Christ. Primarily for this reason, the church has repeatedly questioned its authority. It was not accepted in the East until A.D. 367 under Athanasius, the bishop of Alexandria.[2]

The Jewish character of the book is obvious in several ways. It relies heavily upon earlier Jewish *apocalyptic* texts and end-time scenarios. It uncritically embraces the Jewish vision of an all-powerful and just God ordering violent punishment in judgment against the enemies of God's people and revenge for the suffering of the innocent elect. The merciful, redemptive grace of the God whom Jesus represented and Paul proclaimed seems foreign to the divine character manifest in this series of end-time visions. Like all *apocalyptic* seers before him, the author of Revelation had lost all hope for the world. The world, from his point of view, was beyond redemption.

The Popular Appeal of Revelation

The popularity of the book among people who are disillusioned with the way things are, who suffer for their faith, or who are alienated from the dominant culture, suggests that the author's vision speaks for them. Since the late first century, when it was initially published, it has resonated with communities that have experienced the tensions associated with social, economic, and political upheaval. It gives voice to the angst that people always feel in the face of evil, death, and oppression. It helps in making sense out of otherwise chaotic and meaningless events.

* Reflect on the way that you are personally coping with the current threats to your security and that of your family. To what extent do you ignore the facts in order to carry on with ordinary life? How might it be useful to face the dangers more directly in light of your faith? Begin or renew that process now. If you are keeping a notebook, write your initial reflections on these matters in the form of a prayer.

Even in times of plenty, suffering persists. Evil lurks beneath the surface of things that otherwise appear innocent. Humanity grieves the loss of its Eden. We intuitively abhor the moral and cultural corruption around us, though we may ignore it at a conscious level. What the seer articulates resonates with our preconscious perceptions. Though its language and imagery are strange, it mirrors reality as many experience it.

The author's visions focus readers' attention on the terror they prefer to ignore. Like a nightmare that haunts us in the daytime, Revelation forces us to deal with the intolerable aspects of our world. It describes that which lies beyond language and rational thought, creating a dream-like reality with words. Though the Revelation will forever remain obscure, its images return to us in liturgy, hymnody, and prayer as if to remind us of a lesson we have yet to learn.

The Context of the Revelation

Read the biblical references to visions associated with "vocation" and "revelation": Genesis 40–41; Ezekiel 1:1-3; Isaiah 6:1-8; Daniel 7; Galatians 1:12; 2 Corinthians 12:1-7. Have you ever had an out-of-body experience? What was it like, and what long-term impact did it have on you?

John was exiled to the Isle of Patmos in the Aegean Sea off the coast of Asia Minor in approximately A.D. 95, during the persecution of Christians ordered by the Roman emperor Domitian. John no doubt felt intense anger toward the empire, the unfaithful city of Rome, its wealth and materialism, its moral degradation, and its pagan religion. In isolation, while fasting and praying for an extended period, he found himself in an altered state of consciousness. He testified, "I was in the spirit on the Lord's day" (1:10a). On a Sunday, while in ecstatic prayer, as if standing outside himself, he experienced being led by an angelic vision into a transcendent dimension where he beheld God in Christ and was shown all that was to take place in the near future (1:1-2, 9-13).

> Have you ever fasted long enough to experience a temporarily altered state of consciousness? Learn about the physiological changes that can occur under various forms of stress, particularly as they may affect consciousness and normal thought processes. Use a medical encyclopedia as a resource.

The *mythic* style of the book, replete with other-worldly symbolism, wild beasts, and numerology, set in the context of a God-given disclosure of divinely predetermined events, places the content of the Revelation above rational evaluation. The visionary experience self-authenticates, in a similar way that the visions of *shamans* convey healing power within primitive religious communities. This high regard for messages received through visions and dreams is a cross-cultural and ancient phenomenon. Joseph had divinely inspired prophetic dreams and could interpret them (Genesis 37:5-9; chapters 40–41). Hebrew priests would go through a seven-day fast prior to ordination, during which they were expected to experience a vision and, through the vision, their divine call (see Ezekiel 1:1-3). A parallel to the priestly experience is the prophetic call received by way of a vision, as illustrated by Isaiah 6:1-8 and

> Whether or not you have experienced a vision or other mystical event, interview someone who has. Encourage the person to describe what he or she saw or heard. What insights do you have into the nature and function of such religious experiences?

Daniel 7. The apostle Paul reported several visionary experiences, most importantly the revelation of the exalted Christ and the disclosure of his gospel (Galatians 1:12; 2 Corinthians 12:1-7). A message received by way of a heavenly vision leaves an indelible mark on the seer. The profound impact of the vision discourages careful analysis.

The underlying assumption of such a mystical journey is that, in a three-tiered universe, God takes counsel with angelic beings in the heav-

> * Which form of intelligence do you regard as more authoritative: intuitive or analytical? Does what you know from experience have more or less influence on you than something that you have been taught or that you have read about? Which form of intelligence dominates in revelation received through dreams or visions and reported through an *apocalypse*? Why? Read Revelation 1:3; 22:18-19.

ens to determine actions to be taken on the earth below. Thus, history is predetermined. The rare visitor to the heavenly domain can be guided by a divine messenger and thus come to know in advance an otherwise undisclosed truth, or the future before it unfolds. By way of such a journey, and through the insights given by angelic interpretation, the *prophet* reports information based on what is commonly regarded as the highest form of inspiration. The visions are recorded as entirely trustworthy and binding, never to be altered, and to be read aloud with great reverence in the congregation of the saints (Revelation 1:1-3; 22:18-19).

The Content and Impact of the Vision

A reading of *the Revelation to John* calls forth hope for the ultimate redemption of creation in the form of a new heaven and new earth (21:1–22:5). Its images of a new Jerusalem and of the marriage supper of the Lamb echo classic themes of divine blessing for the faithful in a future state, including bodily resurrection, reunion with all the saints, and the ecstasy of everlasting life in the presence of the Lord (19:7-8). The vision inspires hope for justice with eternal punishment for the unrighteous and the ultimate defeat of evil. In addition, the vision pre-

> * Read Revelation 21:1–22:5. How is the vision of the New Jerusalem like the original paradise of the garden of Eden, and how is it different from it? What does this say about the *prophet's* perception of the natural world?

dicts terrible suffering and the destruction of the physical world. It has been called a form of constructive pessimism. The impact of the vision upon the reader may include serious motivation to reexamine one's life and to pursue personal holiness in the hope of avoiding eternal punishment. While the visions of punishment enhance awareness of the consequences of greed, self-indulgence, materialism, and apostasy, the heavenly anthems sung by the saints and angels inspire our awe and suggest transcendent beauty (4:8, 11; 5:12; 7:12; 11:15-18; 15:3-4; 19:1-8). Worshipers singing or reading these passages can find themselves adoring the holy and being sanctified in submission to the authority of the revelation and of the Christ, in concert with the original seer. The reader experiences a divine perspective on reality.

> Read Revelation 4:8, 11; 5:12; 7;12; 11:15-18; 15:3-4; 19:1-8; 21:1–22:5. Search your hymnal for songs, hymns, and spiritual songs that maintain the impact of *the Revelation to John.* Refer to the section in the hymnal that functions as an index of Scripture references. Select one hymn from the list, and consider its impact on you and your congregation. When and how is it used effectively? Make a journal entry about your reflections, plan to lead your group in song or prayer using this resource, or begin planning a worship/devotional time based on these materials.

Tribulation and the Millennial Reign

Echoing earlier *apocalypses*, Revelation predicts a long period of *tribulation* during which the faithful will be sealed against destruction. According to the vision, an angel declares, "Do not damage the earth or the sea or the trees, until we have marked the servants of our God with a seal on their foreheads" (Revelation 7:3; also, Ezekiel 9:3-10). The number of the elect is to be 144,000, a symbolic number representing a divinely predetermined multitude of the redeemed, none of whom will be ultimately lost or destroyed (Revelation 7:4).

A sustained debate has taken place among believers as to the meaning of Revelation 7:3 and whether God will protect the righteous faithful from suffering during this time of trouble. The dominant view among *mainstream scholars* holds that God will preserve the faithful from judgment, but not insulate them from suffering (see 1 Corinthians 10:13; Mark 13:19-27).

> * Read Revelation 7:3; also, Ezekiel 9:3-10. How are these texts similar? What influence might Ezekiel have had on John? Now read Revelation 7:3-8. (See also 1 Corinthians 10:6-13.) What is your understanding of the seal of protection and of those who receive it?

> * Read Revelation 6:9-11; 7:3, 13-14; and 20:4-6. How do these passages relate to one another and interpret one another? What message do they convey?

In fact, many will be martyred (Revelation 6:9-11; 7:13-14; also, Daniel 12:1). A further detail of the vision indicates that the martyrs will be raised from the dead in a first resurrection, at the coming of Christ to reign for a thousand years (Revelation 20:4-6).

Another significant and often debated feature of John's Apocalypse is something frequently referred to as "the *millennial reign*." Revelation promises a thousand-year reign of Christ, during which the righteous martyrs will serve as judges, sharing the authority of their Lord to rule the nations. At the close of that ideal era, Satan will be released from the underworld to terrorize the earth but will later be defeated and banished to everlasting torment with all his followers. Only after that final battle between God and Satan will the *general resurrection* of the dead occur and a new heaven and a new earth emerge (21:1–22:5).

Thinking Critically About the Revelation

> * Read Revelation 19; Romans 12:19; and Matthew 5:44-48. Now read Revelation 2:27; 12:5; 19:15; also, Isaiah 11:4b; compare and contrast Luke 22:24-30. How are "revenge" and "justice" related but different from each other? How did Jesus expect to exercise his power in the Kingdom? Begin now to compare and contrast the character of the reigning Lord in Revelation with that of Jesus of Nazareth. Record your insights.

Upon careful examination, some scholars believe that they can identify clear psychological dynamics, as well as historical and social motivations, behind the visionary experience reported by the seer. The powerful supernatural medium by which the message is conveyed justifies the pre-conscious, vengeful energy of both the *prophet* and his disciples by projecting these impulses onto God (Revelation 19). By envisioning the wrath of God justly expressed in the violent punishment of evildoers, the seer and his disciples avoid any moral accountability for the way they feel about their enemies (compare and contrast Romans 12:19 and Matthew 5:44-48). The Lord is pictured as pouring out wrath and ruling with a rod of iron, thus satisfying the need of the reader for vindication and empowerment (Revelation 2:27; 12:5; 19:15; also, Isaiah 11:4b; compare and contrast Luke 22:24-27). Adela Yarbro Collins suggests that Revelation serves a cathartic function, purging the reader of fears and resentment and removing their painful or disquieting elements, much as Greek tragedies did for their public.[3]

The Enduring Value of Revelation

The spirit that John awaited and welcomed so enthusiastically came as a voice of comfort in the midst of powerlessness and humiliation. His *beatific vision*, received as he overheard conversations in the throne room of God, provided the much-sought-after consolation of the saints. It served as a breakthrough experience by which John could transcend his confinement and his anger, sublimating them in ecstasy, worship, and pastoral writing on behalf of his persecuted brothers and sisters in Christ.

Undoubtedly the seer felt the perversity of his times more acutely than did most of his contemporaries. While many were lulled into moral complacency and tolerance by the necessity to adapt to their environment, John foresaw the inevitable consequences of Rome's lust for power and its greed. He portrayed the future with word pictures that seem *hyperbolic*, if not horrific. Nonetheless, his intuition and his passion serve as a clarion call in any era of moral confusion, political corruption, and material abundance. The *prophet* warned the churches to purify themselves, to endure, and to remain faithful in the midst of intensifying trouble.

> What parallels do you see between Rome at the close of the first century and first-world nations in the early twenty-first century? Create a collage of images that depicts your insights.

Perhaps Revelation should be read as one would meditate before an icon. The Christian reader, out of respect for the seer and his work, can bring sympathetic understanding to Revelation, informed by knowledge of the historical context, the *prophet's* struggle to remain faithful in the midst of devastation and danger, and his longing for communion with God. Just as a painted icon is only a bridge for transcendence in worship and not itself to be believed or worshiped, so also the recorded vision of the seer is a bridge to cross over with humility, love, imagination, faith, and hope.

Closing

Sing a hymn derived from the Book of Revelation, based on your survey, or sing, "Hail, Thou Once Despised Jesus" or "For the Healing of the Nations." Sing and pray the Lord's Prayer in at least two forms.

Offer one another the parting blessing: *The peace of the Lord be with you. And also with you.*

Revelation must never be reduced to certain theological or spiritual principles. Neither can it be understood as having been fulfilled in the second or the fifth or any other century. It continues to be fulfilled as believers, seekers, and the church approach the vision faithfully, experiencing its drama, chaos, strangeness, conflict, glory, horror, and triumph.

Revelation is a reflection of the various discordant dimensions of reality, both past and present, both known and hoped for. It is to be felt and intuited, rather than analyzed or decoded. It suggests a response that can have transformational impact on the believing community and can, in turn, lead toward the kingdom of God on earth as it is in heaven.

Notes

1. *The New Oxford Annotated Bible*, Bruce Metzger and Roland Murphy, editors; New York: Oxford University Press, 1994; page 364.

2. Roland H. Bainton, *Christendom, Vol. I*; New York: Harper & Row, 1966; page 69.

3. Arthur W. Wainwright, *Mysterious Apocalypse: Interpreting the Book of Revelation*; Eugene, Oregon: Wipf and Stock Publishers, 2001; pages 150–51.

For More Information

Read your church's doctrinal statement about the justification of the sinner. How does this doctrine address the current discussion about readying ourselves for the close of the age and our expectations of last things?

Review the historic confessions of faith, doctrinal standards, and religious practices of your denomination for any reference to the Final Judgment and to escaping condemnation. What important practical function does this material serve in the life of the church? What enduring message does this end-time warning convey?

Use your public library to learn more about "*shamans*" and their usual means of receiving visions and instruction on behalf of their communities.

Read about the *mythology* of other cultures and religions as it pertains to the beginning of history and its end. Compare Jewish/Christian *apocalyptic* with what you discover.

Take a tour of a nearby city with an eye for evidence of parallels between late first-century Rome and U.S. civilization today.

Visit a museum of modern art. Consider the expressions of sculptors and painters as possible visual *apocalypses*. What do you see? What are these artists saying about our world?

Visit a Greek or Russian Orthodox home or sanctuary. Experience an icon and learn about the use of these traditional images in worship and prayer. How might Revelation serve a parallel function?

CHAPTER 6
END-TIME TEACHINGS

The History of Christian Eschatology After A.D. 70

Focus
The history of Christian hope for the reign of Christ on earth

The destruction of Jerusalem and the Temple radically altered the worldview and religion of both Jews and Jewish Christians. It seems that prior to and during that war many thought the end of the world had come. Their teachers worked hard to contain the hysteria and interpret the events as but a prelude to the end. What had occurred in Palestine, they believed, was not the end but part of the increasing trouble that *prophecy* foretold would precede the end.

Gathering

Greet one another with the words, "Grace and peace to you in our Lord Jesus." If you have brought a hymn to sing from the teaching/learning exercises, lead it. Otherwise, sing "O Holy City Seen of John." If you have experienced the Spirit speaking to you through your study in a redeeming way, briefly share your witness of faith. Share one another's joys and concerns, and pray for one another. Close your gathering time with the prayer for illumination from Psalm 43:3, followed by a few moments of silent listening for God:

O send out your light and your truth;
let them lead me;
let them bring me to your holy hill
and to your dwelling. Amen.

Jews and Christians fled the burning city. The war and the loss of the Temple led to the close of an era in Jewish history. The Sanhedrin met in exile in Jamnia, four miles from the Mediterranean Sea and just north-north-east of Ashdod, until the Second Revolt in A.D. 132. In A.D. 100, Jewish leaders gathered there to formally establish the canon of the Hebrew Scriptures and, for all practical purposes, invent Judaism. Israel would no longer be understood as

> * Have you ever felt or thought that the end of the world might be coming soon? Do you know someone who responded to WWII, the Cuban Missile Crisis, the Gulf War, or 9/11 in this way? How do these fears affect beliefs and the practice of faith?

a sacred political entity with a homeland. Instead, Israel was reconceived as the dispersed people of God united in the study of Torah, the Prophets, and the Writings, as well as in the practice of a historic tradition. *Apocalypticism* continued to influence Jewish thought well into the second century, due to upheaval, alienation, and fear among Jews and Jewish Christians.

A Shift in Focus–Divergent Interpretations of the Christian Hope

As the Gentile Christian mission gained momentum and integrated elements of Greek and Roman philosophy into its message, the Jewish Christian churches that had deep roots in the Hebrew Scriptures abandoned hope for this world and looked toward a clearly and solely divine intervention in the *Parousia*. Even though Rome appeared to rule, the church believed that God remained *sovereign* and would exercise saving power in the near future.

The Gentile Christian communities also maintained an *eschatological vision*, although their focus was on proclaiming the message throughout the world. The church came to believe and teach that its message must be preached to all nations before the end would come. Faithfulness in *evangelism*

> * When you think of your future with God, do you think first of heaven or of the kingdom of God on earth in your lifespan? Which is more compelling or real to you? Why? Which is more frequently reflected in the worship life of your congregation? Pay close attention to the prayers, hymns, and anthems as you formulate your conclusion. What difference does it make?

Restate in your own words the four major approaches to the truth of Jesus' proclamation, "The kingdom of God is at hand": political, ecclesiastical, communitarian or utopian, and mystical. Give an example of each, either from the textbook or from your contemporary experience of the church and its faith in action. Which of these do you consider the most reliable?

would shorten the time of persecution and trouble. It would hasten the coming of the Lord.

Most of the *early church fathers* taught that *the Revelation to John* had begun to be fulfilled during the period of the historical Jesus and continued to be realized in events immediately preceding the vision itself, as well as in events that developed during the second and third centuries. They looked particularly to Rome, with its seven hills, as being the Babylon of Revelation 17 and 18 and saw in the persecution by the emperor Nero, who was finally killed in battle, the historical reality of the wounded beast of Revelation (Revelation 13:3 and 17:8).[1] Popular belief held that Nero would rise again, following this mortal blow, to further persecute the church. The *early church fathers* found in this legend the prototype for the vision of John the Revelator that foresaw the resurrection of the beast to further torment God's people. Fear of persecution, violence due to attacks on the Empire, and divisions among Christians fueled the Revelation, they taught, and gave it historical meaning. The early church believed that it was living in the midst of the final *tribulation*.

Find an example of each of the four major interpretations of the Kingdom in your hymnal. Evaluate the usefulness and limitations of each vision, and consider when and how these hymns are used within your faith community. Is the political vision used on occasions closely related to national holidays? If so, what does this say about your congregation's understanding of the relationship between the kingdom of God and the nation-state? Which of the four hymn types might best be described as the "heart music" of your church?

Only gradually did the apocalyptic worldview yield to alternatives. Among them was pursuit of immortality for the soul beyond death, as climaxed in Dante's *Divine Comedy* (composed ca. 1307–1315). Over several centuries, beginning in the late first century, various this-worldly applications of Jesus' proclamation of the imminent kingdom of God took root and shaped faith, as well, including communitarian, mystical, political, and ecclesiastical interpretations.

The political interpretation of the kingdom of God waited for Constantine and the mid-fourth-century A.D. Constantine ended persecution of Christians and created a close allegiance between the church and the state in order to unify his empire. In doing so, he established a standard for orthodox Christianity, based largely on political considerations, through the Council of Nicea. It was Augustine, however, who first clearly articulated the political reinterpretation of Christian *eschatology* in *The City of God* (circa A.D. 400) as a critique of the empire. During the Middle Ages, when church and state collaborated as partners in the Holy Roman Empire, particularly under Charlemagne, it was often intimated that the *millennial reign* of Christ on earth was underway. The state derived its authority to rule from the heavenly kingdom of God and sought to implement canon law in the secular realm. Byzantine Christianity would offer an ecclesiastical vision of the kingdom of God: the institutional church as the realized kingdom of God or present millennial reign of Christ on earth (fifth century; also, Revelation 20:2-7).

Myriad utopian communities and separatist groups would experiment, over the course of twenty centuries, with living according to the teachings of Christ as colonies of heaven on earth, deriving much of their inspiration from Revelation. The proponents of each application of the faith believed that they were the righteous followers of Christ on earth, preparing for or participating in his *millennial reign.*

The loss of Jerusalem as a physical place led to hopes for a New Jerusalem in the heavens and to an increasingly metaphorical reference to Jerusalem in liturgy and prayer (Revelation 21:1–22:5). Origen (ca. A.D. 185–254) was a strong advocate of a spiritual rather than a material interpretation of the New Jerusalem portrayed in Revelation.[2] Believers increasingly placed their hope in life beyond death, rather than in peace with justice among nations within the context of history: "We look for the resurrection of the dead, and for the life of the world to come" (Nicene Creed, A.D. 381).

Others, beginning with *Gnostic* groups (late first century and second century A.D.), sought transcendent experiences of the glorious Christ through contemplative prayer and ritualized piety. These practices led some to much prized mystical experiences and what the *Gnostics* called "knowledge." Although the *early church fathers* deemed the many forms of *Gnosticism* heretical, active *apocalyptic* expectation gradually yielded to regularized liturgical practices in the church at large.

> * Reread Revelation 20:2-8 for familiarity.
> Read it again interpreting it literally, as if following a narrative outline of events. Paraphrase what you believe the author says will happen.
> Review the passage as if the intention of the passage is metaphorical. What does the metaphor suggest?
> Finally, consider the text while listening for a theological principle. Formulate a statement of the underlying truth of the passage. Of these three approaches to hearing the Word of God through the passage, which seems most true to the Spirit and message of Jesus? Which seems most true to the intention of the author?

Many believers relied on a current and active relationship with Jesus Christ for their sense of hope. They attempted to enjoy eternal life in the present, thereby tasting in advance that which lay ahead. They often understood this to be possible only by transcending bodily existence. While they sought spiritual communion with the risen Lord through the Holy Spirit, the liturgy and the sacraments of the church, the faithful continued to confess, "He [Christ] will come again in glory to judge the living and the dead, and his kingdom will have no end" (Nicene Creed).

The Millennium in Christian Thought

Revelation 20:2-7 has spawned a long history of theological discussion and debate. Moreover, it inspired a plethora of visions for a coming perfect age. Out of these verses emerged a strong expectation on the part of many for a thousand-year reign of Christ on earth, usually referred to as the *millennial reign* or the *millennium*, during which Satan shall be banished and unadulterated righteousness, peace, and abundance are to be enjoyed by the faithful, including the resurrected martyrs. The relationship between the second coming of Christ and the *millennium* has been variously understood as being *premillennial, postmillennial,* or *amillennial,* a coming that is disassociated from expectations of a *millennial reign* on earth.

> * Read Revelation 3:3; 17 (especially verse 8); and 18. Which seems more likely to you: (1) these visions were stimulated by current events and fears; (2) these visions predict the distant future?

Amillennialism

Basing his teaching largely on the Gospel of John, Origen (A.D. 185–254) taught that the *millennium* began with Jesus' death and resurrection. The souls of the righteous would go to paradise with Christ upon death, where they would be prepared for heaven, while awaiting the *general resurrection.*[3] Everett Ferguson regards Origen's theories as a "spiritualizing interpretation of Revelation and the millennium."[4] He says that most early Christians in the first three centuries were *amillennial* in their view of history. They did not expect a literal reign of Christ on earth for a thousand years.[5] They believed that good and evil co-exist within history and that the reign of Christ exists outside of history until the Second Coming and the Final Judgment.

Augustine of Hippo (A.D. 354–430), an *amillennialist,* interpreted Revelation 20 as describing the reign of the church until the *Parousia.* Augustine had been heavily influenced in his thinking about the *millennium* by the fourth-century theologian, Tyconius. He interpreted the reference to a one-thousand-year period as symbolic of completion, rather than as a literal date or period of years.

In place of a *millennial reign, amillennialists* looked for an other-worldly *eschatological* realization of the kingdom of God. It should be noted that after Augustine, *premillennialism* virtually died in the West, not to be revived until the seventeenth century under the leadership and interpretative influences of the Reformers.

> * Would you describe yourself as postmillennial, premillennial, or amillennial in your view of the future and the coming of Christ? Why?

Even without confidence in an earthly *millennium,* however, expectations of the *eschaton,* including the resurrection of the dead and a final judgment, as well as belief in heaven and hell remained vivid among the *amillennialists.*[6]

During the medieval period, calculations of the age of the earth based on Revelation were popular. Many taught that the earth was six thousand years old and would enjoy a thousand-year sabbath. Augustine and the Venerable Bede offered spiritual interpretations of the *millennium,* so as to quiet *apocalyptic* speculation while encouraging expectations of an imminent Second Coming and Day of Judgment.[7] Romanesque and Gothic church architecture and art reveal an *amillennial* view of the reigning Christ who comes to execute the judgment of all souls, suggesting the broad cultural impact of the teachings of Augustine and Bede.[8]

Thomas Aquinas (1225–1274) regarded *millennialism* as heresy. Nonetheless, saints and mystics continued to receive visions and offer prophetic messages that indicated the nearness of the *apocalypse*. For example, Hildegaard of Bingen, a German abbess, published her predictions of the end of history. The Roman Catholic order organized around Francis of Assisi believed their founder to be an *apocalyptic* figure, perhaps the angel of Revelation 7:2.[9] The habit of contemplative prayer, and other mystical means of communion with God, led many who were so inclined to rapturous revelation and, with it, certainty of the imminence of the Kingdom.

Postmillennialism

Somewhere in every generation, and particularly during the eighteenth and nineteenth centuries, groups of believers emerged around the *postmillennial* belief that their particular movement represented the crucial divine activity by which the *millennium* was being realized, after which Christ will return bodily. Rather than living in the midst of the final *tribulation,* they believed they lived in the *millennial reign* of Christ and were the evidence of Christ's supreme authority on earth. Among the groups who embraced this *postmillennial* interpretation of Revelation were the Montanists (ca. A.D. 160); Joachites (sixteenth century); the Millerites or Seventh Day Adventists (who once dated the Second Coming at October 22, 1844); the Disciples of Christ; followers of Alexander Campbell (1788–1866); the Oneida Community of Putney, Vermont, under the leadership of John H. Noyes (1811–1886); the Aurora Colony of Oregon under William Keil (1812–1877); the Shakers under Ann Lee (1736–1784); the Mennonites led by Menno Simons (1496–1561); the Proselytes (Taze Russell, 1852–1916) or Jehovah's Witnesses; and the Mormons inspired by Joseph Smith (1805–1844), as well as myriad less well known sects and cults, monastic groups, and utopian communities. In every case these hopes have proved illusive and disappointing.

The famous American theologian and

> Search your hymnal, older hymnals, and collections of plain song for hymns composed and made popular during one of the two Great Awakenings, 1730's and 1880's. What *millennial* themes surface? Characterize the spiritual motivations of the period. Select a hymn to present to your group in a creative format.

philosopher, Jonathan Edwards (1703–1758), believed that the religious awakening occurring in New England gave evidence of the in-breaking *millennium*. Some believe that his preaching and writing encouraged the Revolutionary War and United States independence. George Whitefield (1714–1770) and Charles Finney (1792–1875), major leaders in the first and second Great Awakenings respectively, also subscribed to the *millennial* vision and were *postmillennialist* in their expectations for the coming of Christ. They taught that God ruled through rational means and would not intervene in catastrophic, nonrational ways. The eighteenth-century *postmillennial* revivals led to increased missionary activity and an enthusiastic confidence that civilization was progressing toward the fulfillment of the reign of Christ on earth.

The optimism relative to a gradual emergence of the *millennial reign* through spiritual revival and the American experiment led most Protestants in the United States before the Civil War, however, to be relatively passive regarding social justice issues such as slavery, women's rights, alcohol use and abuse, the alleviation of poverty, and prison reform. Eventually the religious fervor yielded to more secular theories of human progress throughout the Civil War years and into the twentieth century. The World Wars and the Great Depression, during the first half of the new century, would silence the optimism of both the *postmillennialists* and the later social gospel movement. They would yield their influence to *fundamentalism* and a resurgent *premillennialism*.

Premillennialism

The *early church father,* Papias (A.D. 60–ca. 130), first articulated the doctrine of *premillennialism*, as reported by the historian Eusebius in the fourth century.[10] He taught that Christ would return before the *millennial reign* on earth began. Justin Martyr (ca. A.D. 100–ca. 165) followed suit, embracing the perspective in the mid-second century. Irenaeus (ca. A.D. 130–ca. 200) and Tertullian (A.D. 160–ca. 225), Hippolytus (ca. 170–ca. 230), Victorinus (d. A.D. 304), Lactantius (ca. 240–ca. 320), Methodius (d. 311), and Commodianus (third century A.D) continued their work.[11] They predicted a time of intense conflict, however, preceding the *millennium*. According to Justin Martyr, the timeline for these *apocalyptic* events would include the resurrection of the righteous, a thousand years of abundance to be enjoyed by the righteous in their resurrected bodies (per Irenaeus), followed by the *general resurrection* and the Final Judgment.[12]

73

Resistance Movements

The Book of Revelation served as a source of negative rhetorical language as well as inspiration for *millennial* claims. During the seventh century, Christian writers drew on *apocalyptic* language to demonize Muslim invaders, identifying them as the anti-Christ and his warriors. In the thirteenth century, critics of the papacy reinterpreted Revelation and used it to demonize the pope.

> Do you know people who are so alienated from organized Christianity that they believe the church to be a force for evil? If possible, interview one or more of these people. What validity do you find in their perspective?

Many saw Rome and the pope as the beast of Revelation. Numerous sects emerged in resistance to the wealth and corruption of the papacy and in an effort to recover New Testament Christianity. Among them was the movement spawned by Joachim of Fiore, who divided history into three ages: the first, the Age of the Father; the second, the Age of the Son; and the third, the Age of the Spirit. Fiore subdivided each age into seven others. He believed that his own era fell into the Age of the Son, just prior to the beginning of the Age of the Spirit,

> What is the history of anti-Roman Catholic sentiment in your area? In what way is it related or unrelated to *millennial* thought? What is its origin and motivation?

which he expected to be inaugurated in 1260. He based his prediction on an obscure passage in Revelation (Revelation 12:6). With the coming of the Age of the Spirit, the visible church would be dissolved, and with it the papacy.[13]

Protestants revisited this doctrine of the end times, beginning with the work of Joseph Mede (1586–1638). *Premillennialism* enjoyed a significant revival in England in the 1820's and was popularized by the work of J. Nelson Darby in the United States, especially between 1820 and 1877. During this time, the Civil War was seen by many as the necessary purging that would usher in the *millennium*.[14] These Protestants held, however, that only the intervention of Christ could

> Is there any residual sentiment in your region regarding the Civil War as a fulfillment of the purgative work of God? Why does such sentiment persist? Study the "Battle Hymn of the Republic" for this theme. Why is this hymn popular today?

establish the kingdom of God on earth. No human effort, including war, could inaugurate a new age. Out of Darby's work came the modern *dispensationalist* movement that influenced the worldview of fully a quarter of the U.S. population by the close of the twentieth century.

The Rise of Fundamentalism

The *premillennialism* that Darby spawned found favor among North Americans who were engaged in a resistance movement against the encroaching modernism of Protestant Christianity. They favored a literal interpretation of all Scripture, believing it to be inerrant and in no case self-contradictory. Theologians from Princeton Theological Seminary, most notably the *postmillennialist* Charles Hodge (1797–1878), also fostered a fundamentalist perspective on history and biblical interpretation. Although Hodge preferred to understand biblical *prophecy* as designed to "keep the faith of the people of God alive and 'not to anticipate history,' "insisting that "it is not 'intended to enable them to see the chronological order of events by which they were to be accomplished,' "he nonetheless aligned himself with Darby and his followers in insisting on a biblical interpretation of reality over against the scientific rationalism that was increasingly popular following Darwin's publication of *The Origin of the Species*.[15] The Princetonians joined ranks with the *premillennialists* in the fight to preserve the authority of the Bible against the onslaught of secularism.[16]

Fundamentalism emerged within Protestant Christianity as a popular movement in the 1920's and became a significant force in North American culture by the mid-1940's. It provided a strong voice for an interventionist understanding of God and actively opposed the Gospel of Progress or Social Gospel, espoused by mainline Protestantism of the same period. The Movement reasserted the biblical teaching that only God can save. The rise of the Pentecostal Movement paralleled the rise of *fundamentalism* and was itself an *eschatological* faith based on *biblical literalism*.

Both movements provided a firm ground for faith, allowed for little freedom of interpretation, and fostered sharp dichotomies relative to God and the devil, good and evil, heaven and hell, and the "saved" and the "unsaved." These increasingly important expressions of Christianity took evil seriously and reestablished, on biblical foundations, powerful and ultimate sanctions against it, emphasizing the reality of sin, Satan, judgment, and eternal damnation. Both the fundamentalists and the

Pentecostal churches ultimately set aside Charles Hodge's more liberal biblical *hermeneutic* and *postmillennial* interpretation of Revelation in favor of *biblical literalism* and the *dispensationalist* conceptualization of *prophecy* and history.

Dispensationalism

Darby, and his fundamentalist followers, relied heavily on what they believed to be a rational and scientific system of biblical interpretation that "proved" *prophecy*. The plethora of charts and graphs and the movement's reliance on the methodology of Francis Bacon illustrates their application of the scientific method to biblical interpretation.[17] Among the most prominent of the cartographers of the biblical past, present, and future was Clarence Larkin.[18] Out of this movement came a "philosophy of history" that "accounted for the place of the church within biblical revelation," says James Callahan, writing for *Fides et Historia: Journal for the Conference on Faith and History*.[19] The *dispensationalists* made a critical differentiation between the role of the Jews and that of the Christian church in the fulfillment of Revelation. While the "saved" constitute the new Israel of God, the reestablishment of the nation of Israel, with Jerusalem as its capital, is crucial, they believe, to the return of Christ.

> Look at the chart in the appendix (page 112). Compare them with the timelines that you have created in studying *apocalyptic* thought. What similarities and differences do you notice?

The movement insists that all history is divinely predetermined and forecast by Revelation. As Darby had taught, so they believed: "Prophecy records things to come. It is the scriptural mirror wherein future events are seen."[20] Much like Joachim of Fiore in the thirteenth century, the Darbyites teach that history has been divinely organized into seven distinct "dispensations" or eras.[21] They use current events to verify the timeliness of biblical *prophecies* and to enhance a sense of urgency to prepare for the events soon to come.

In Summary

The history of Christian thought documents the persistent influence that *apocalyptic* expectation has had. Hope for the ultimate defeat of evil and the fulfillment of God's reign has fueled myriad efforts to cooperate with

76

God in bringing this hope into the realm of historical reality. While the philosophical and theological lenses through which Christians interpret Scripture greatly affect their vision of the kingdom of God, Christians have always watched for the return of Christ. Widespread interest in end-time teaching

Closing
Sing the hymn, "Be Thou My Vision." Pray for the church. Offer one another a closing blessing:

The peace of the Lord be with you. And also with you.

indicates the resonance between traditional Christian *eschatology* and the pervasive human need to trust in the goodness of a powerful God who will redeem the world and bring its often-tragic history to glorious resolution.

Notes

1. Wainwright, page 26.

2. Wainwright, page 30.

3. Everett Ferguson, "Millennial and Amillennial Expectations in Christian Eschatology," in Loren L. Johns, editor, *Apocalypticism and Millennialism*; Kitchener, Ontario: Pandora Press, 2000; pages 140–41.

4. Ibid., page 141.

5. Ibid., page 129.

6. Ibid., pages 146–47.

7. Ibid., page 149.

8. Ibid., page 151.

9. Ibid., pages 151, 155.

10. Eusebius, *Church History,* 3:39.11–13.

11. Ferguson, page 133 in *Apocalypticism and Millennialism*; Arthur W. Wainwright, *Mysterious Apocalypse*, page 23.

12. Ferguson, page 134.

13. Roland H. Bainton, *Christendom, Vol. I*; New York: Harper, 1966; page 217.

14. Charles B. Strozier, *Apocalypse: On the Psychology of Fundamentalism*; Boston: Beacon Press, 1944; pages 168–81.

15. Joe L. Coker, *Fides et Historia*, Journal of the Conference on Faith and History, Vol. XXX:I Winter/Spring, 1998; page 49.

16. Coker, pages 48–56.

17. Strozier, pages 183, 184.

18. *Dispensational Truth or God's Plan and Purpose in the Ages*, self-published, 1918.

19. XXVIII:1 Winter/Spring 1996, page 81.

20. John Nelson Darby, *The Hopes of the Church of God in Connexion with the Destiny of the Jews and the Nations as Revealed in Prophecy*, 1841, pages 167–68; as cited by Coker in *Fides et Historia*, XXX:1, page 51.

21. Larkin, *Dispensational Truth.*

For More Information

Find an example of a church or community in your region that subscribes to the *premillennial* worldview and interpretation of Scripture. Learn all that you can about their way of life and attitudes toward those who do not subscribe to their beliefs and practices.

Select one of the *postmillennial* movements in the United States and learn how they moved from predicting a particular date for the *second coming of Christ*, through disappointment, toward becoming a more enduring faith community. How did the movement succeed or fail? Why?

Reread the Gospel of John with an eye for more deeply understanding its *eschatology*.

Interview someone from a contemplative religious order who may be able to offer insight into the role of mysticism in creating a vital *eschatology* for Roman Catholics. As an alternative, interview an active charismatic Christian or Pentecostal believer who can help you know more about the visions and dreams of Christian *prophets* today.

CHAPTER 7
END-TIME TEACHINGS

The Rapture of the Saints

One of the most beloved promises of *dispensationalist* teaching regarding the end time is the "*rapture* of the church." The term *rapture* refers to the ecstasy that Christians anticipate in being united with

Focus
The doctrine of the rapture

Gathering

Greet one another with the words, "Grace and peace to you in our Lord Jesus."

Sing "Shall We Gather at the River."

Spend some time preparing for meditation by setting aside all books and other study materials, seating yourselves in upright positions, relaxing your bodies, and breathing regularly. Spend three to five minutes with eyes closed focused on the hope of one day being physically in the presence of the risen and reigning Lord. Allow the hope to become more than a visual image. Press into its essence. Allow yourself to become one with the presence of Christ. Seek to dwell in the presence of God. When you have completed your meditation, note how your experience has affected you.

Close with the following response taken from Revelation 21:23; 22:5; 20b:

Leader: God's glory will be our light, and night shall be no more.
Group: Amen. Come, Lord Jesus! Come!

> * What do you think and feel about heaven or about seeing the Lord? Write a poem or make a journal entry that expresses your reflections.

Christ at his appearing. The doctrine holds that the faithful will be caught up in the air to be with the Lord in the heavens, before the great *tribulation*. While J. Nelson Darby may have originated the popular use of *rapture* and formulated it based on his reading of key New Testament passages, the origins of the concept lie in earlier efforts to grapple with the future in light of *apocalyptic prophecy*.

Early Sources of the Doctrine of Rapture

Cotton and Increase Mather, seventeenth-century Puritan preachers from New England, introduced *premillennial* thinking to the new world. Increase Mather (1639–1723) "wrote of the earth's coming destruction by fire, and cited scriptures proving that the saints would be *'caught up into the Air'* beforehand, thereby escaping the final conflagration—an early formulation of the Rapture doctrine," according to Paul Boyer in his work, *When Time Shall Be No More*.[1] Others had proposed similar ideas, but the *premillennial dispensationalist* interpretation of history espoused, preached, and published by Darby made the *doctrine of the rapture* widely available, as early as 1820. Boyer writes, "In a sense, Darby's system contained nothing new. . . . Premillennialism had been an option for Protestant evangelicals since Joseph Mede's day, while rudimentary forms of 'dispensationalism' go back at least as far as Joachim of Fiore. Even Rapture doctrine, as we have seen, can be found in the writings of earlier interpreters, including Increase Mather. But Darby wove these diverse strands into a tight and cohesive system."[2]

> Turn to your hymnal for images and poetic expressions of heaven. See especially sections on death and eternal life, communion of the saints, return and reign of the Lord, and the completion of creation (the city of God). Choose one hymn that reflects meaning and emotions consonant with your own faith and hope. Meditate on one key metaphor or phrase for several minutes.

Defining the Doctrine

Darby, formerly a cleric of the Anglican Church of Ireland, left that institution to join the Plymouth Brethren, a small anti-establishment denomination. He taught that the true church (the righteous) could expect to be taken up to be with Christ immediately before the seven years of *tribulation* that would precede the *millennial* reign of Christ on earth.[3] The *rapture* would come unexpectedly and would usher in the end times. Darby insisted that "the rapture is not Christ's coming to earth, but rather the church going to Christ."[4] The doctrine relied heavily on its own unique interpretation of Paul's encouragement to the saints regarding the *Parousia* of the Lord, found in 1 Thessalonians 4:16-17:

> What distinction do you make between the membership of institutional churches and the faithful people of God? What determines inclusion among the saints? Do you know of churches, congregations, or communities that consider themselves the "true church" to the exclusion of all others? What motivates them and what defines them as unique?

"For the Lord himself shall descend from heaven with a shout, with the voice of the archangel, and with the trump of God; and the dead in Christ shall rise first: Then we which are alive and remain shall be caught up together with them in the clouds, to meet the Lord in the air: and so shall we ever be with the Lord" (King James Version).

> * Compare Revelation 20:1-6 with Mark 13:9-27. What similarities and differences surface? After a literal reading of both passages, as if they were narrative descriptions of the future, determine what each passage says about the timing of the Lord's receiving the faithful ones to himself.

Weber writes, "Up to the early 1830s, it seems that all futurist premillennialists had seen the rapture in conjunction with the second coming of Christ at the end of the tribulation. But dispensationalists, taking their cues from the creative teaching of John Darby, separated them. At the rapture, they said, Christ will come *for* his saints, and at the second coming, he will come *with* his saints."[5] (See Revelation 20:4-5.)

Their insight was derived chiefly from making a radical distinction between the church and Israel, seeing the church as having a heavenly

> * Read Revelation 7. Note the distinction made between the 144,000 of verse 4 and the innumerable multitude of verse 9. Focus on verses 13-14 and the defining phrase: "These are they who have come out of the great ordeal; they have washed their robes and made them white in the blood of the Lamb." To the best of your ability, determine what this passage might mean in a timeline relative to the "*tribulation,*" the *second coming of Christ,* and the *millennial reign.*

dimension that transcends history.[6] The saints, both living and dead, who have been caught up together in the air represent the church triumphant and glorified. Israel, on the other hand, is both a political state to be restored in the course of end-time events and the people who make up the 144,000 of Revelation 7.

Using the Scientific Method

The *dispensationalists* prided themselves in their use of the scientific method in analyzing biblical *prophecy*. They used their technical skills in interpreting their message. Darby had been trained as a lawyer. Others were mathematicians and engineers. Much of their work is impenetrable to the uninitiated, as is the original material they seek to decode. The charts that Cyrus Scofield published, beginning in 1909, within his *Scofield Reference Bible,* made the *dispensationalist* schema more accessible than it had previously been.

> Look again at the chart on page 112 in the Appendix. Compare the chart with your own reading of the Scripture passages in this session. What is the "scientific method"? Can it be used in the study of biblical *prophecy*? Why or why not?

While the spokespersons and publishers who promoted *dispensationalist* doctrine did so in terms that would be acceptable to those who relied on reason, the insight that led to distinguishing between the future of the church and that of faithful Jews may well have been inspired by ecstatic or charismatic *prophecy* received by other members of the Plymouth Brethren Church.[7] The linear thinking of the *dispensationalist* theorists codified the ecstatic proclamation of those caught up in the *eschatological* experience. More recent apostles of this movement focus on communicating the self-evident truth of the Scriptures to the unlettered masses.

A Second Resurrection

The *doctrine of the rapture* forced the introduction of a second resurrection to the timeline of the biblical future (Revelation 20:5-6). The first resurrection would occur for the saints at the appearing of the Lord to *rapture* his church. (Note that the *dispensationalists* have taken the liberty to broaden the church triumphant to include not only the martyrs and the dead, but all the righteous faithful alive at Christ's appearing; compare Revelation 20:4). The second resurrection is to take place at the close of history and will affect only those who were not among the "raptured" saints. Those raised in the second resurrection will face ultimate judgment and condemnation. Joe L. Coker, a contemporary scholar of end-time teachings, echoed Darby's reasoning when he wrote, "If the dead in Christ remained in their graves until a general resurrection following the millennium, they will not be able to participate in the glory of Christ's thousand year reign."[8] The doctrine overcame a major flaw in the *premillennial* schema.

> * Reread Revelation 20:4-6. How does this *prophecy* relate to the Jewish concept of the general resurrection of the dead at the Last Judgment? Compare 1 Thessalonians 4:16-17.

Tribulation

In Darby's thought, the *tribulation* will last seven years and will represent Satan's rule on the earth. This will fulfill the seventieth week referred to by Daniel.[9] (Also read Daniel 7:25; 9:25; 12:7; Revelation 11:2-3; 12:6, 14; 13:5; Matthew 24:21.) The majority view, among *dispensationalists*, is that the *rapture* will remove Christians from this time of torture and corruption. It offers the promise of escape suggested in Luke 21:36, "Be alert at all times, praying that you may have the strength to escape all these things that will take place, and to stand before the Son of Man." At stake in the debate is whether God is seen as one who preserves the saints through *tribula-*

> * Read and compare Daniel 7:25; 9:25; 12:7; Revelation 11:2-3; 12:6, 14; 13:5; and Matthew 24:21. What similarities and differences do you see in the various end-time predictions, relative to the role of the faithful? What difference does it make to you whether the church escapes the end-time *tribulation* or faithfully survives it?

In your opinion, why do some people avoid thinking and learning about religious beliefs and their sources while others eagerly expose themselves to a liberal education? What is the difference between wisdom and education? What are the advantages and dangers of the "wisdom of this world"? How does a faithful person avoid being influenced by false teaching? Prayerfully read 1 Corinthians 1:18-31.

tion and suffering and protects them from final judgment or rescues them before these things take place.

Disseminating the Dispensationalist Doctrines

Darby's work was furthered by countless later evangelists and preachers, as well as a host of laypeople. Among the many early proponents were the Mennonite preacher, Claass Epp, who anticipated the *rapture* in March of 1889. Sir Robert Anderson, James Brookes, Dwight L. Moody, Cyrus Scofield, Donald Gray Barnhouse, and Charles Fuller were important spokespersons. The movement was fueled by anti-establishment feelings about the institutional churches and by distrust of educated clergy in particular. Dallas Theological Seminary, Philadelphia College of Bible, and Fuller School of Theology, to name a few, have been leading sources of instruction for disseminators of *dispensationalist* theory. Their *premillennial*, pretribulation form of *fundamentalism* seeks to "present clearly and biblically the depth of God's promises for those who call Jesus both their Lord and Christ."[10]

The purpose of much *dispensationalist* literature is to make the truth available to business people, homemakers, and the unchurched (nonprofessional theologians) briefly and in plain language. In every generation since Darby, interpreters have used current events to prove the validity of biblical *prophecy* and to forewarn the faithful of the imminent end of history. The majority of their energy focuses on the confusion that will follow the *rapture*, rather than on the ecstasy of communion with Christ or the details of reigning with him. Their motivation is to inspire fear and repentance, as well as reassurance of a blessed escape from the increasing trouble that has already

Watch the media, including recent religious and secular films, for end-time themes. Compare them with the biblical end-time narratives. If possible, tune in on your radio to a *dispensationalist* preacher. Make some notes about your reaction to the style and content of the message.

begun to surface. A few work diligently to develop communities of people who will be considered fit to reign with Christ upon the inauguration of the kingdom of God on earth. (See Appendix: "An Overview of the Twelve Tribes," page 109.) John Walvoord, Hal Lindsey, and Tim LaHaye are among the most widely read contemporary spokespersons for this set of beliefs. While few of the most influential leaders are regularly assigned pastors, many have built large followings through use of mass media. People of all walks of life and all educational levels number among their adherents.

> Read "An Overview of the Twelve Tribes" in the Appendix. Do you know of a community of people who have separated themselves from mainstream society so as to purify themselves and reestablish a faith community based on the descriptions of the early church found in the Acts of the Apostles? What are the defining marks and aspirations of this community?

Motivations to Believe

Those who subscribe to the *dispensationalist doctrine of the rapture* of the saints are drawn to it for a variety of reasons. By expecting to be a part of the *rapture* of the church, they may avoid death. They can expect to meet their now-deceased loved ones in the air. They can look forward, moreover, to being delivered from their present troubles and can trust that they will not have to endure the intense upheaval that *apocalyptic* prophecy predicts will precede the Day of Judgment.

Dispensationalism and its *hermeneutic*, or approach to biblical interpretation, enable the adherent to sustain confidence in miracles and the supernatural in the face of scientific rationalism and higher criticism in biblical studies. It gives believers a sense of being a part of the divine plan and living within the divine purpose. It seems to bring order and meaning to the otherwise chaotic and unknown future.

The popularity of *dispensationalist* doctrine may reveal a thinly disguised self-interest on the part of the adherents, however, rather than

> What is the difference between meeting the Lord and meeting your deceased loved ones in heaven? What difference do the two expectations make in the faith and hope of the believer? Refer to Matthew 22:23-32; Philippians 1:21-23; and 3:13-14.

85

> *** What is the difference between a belief in certain doctrines and trust in God? What is the foundation of your spiritual security?**
>
> **Do you know people who aren't sure what they think about various orthodox Christian beliefs but nevertheless consider themselves Christians? How do people live with skepticism and still enjoy a satisfying spiritual life?**
>
> **How do you understand the reign of Christ and the power of God in light of the tragedies of the twentieth and twenty-first centuries?**

sacred truth. Believers need to believe that their God remains *sovereign* in spite of the apparently tragic events of a long history of waiting and watching for divine intervention. They need an inalienable foundation upon which to build spiritual and intellectual security, as well as an inviolate community of faith. They want reassurance that they will be included among the righteous, that they will be vindicated, and that their adversaries will suffer justice at the hands of God.

Questionable Assumptions

The *dispensationalist* worldview relies on a number of theological assumptions. Chief among them are *theological determinism* and *biblical inerrancy*. *Dispensationalists* believe that God has determined in advance what will take place and has reported it accurately through the biblical *prophets*. The *prophets* have foreseen that which is already in the mind of God, whether God has willed it so or merely anticipated what will result from the pattern of human behavior.

Determinism: This prescientific set of beliefs, suggesting that God looks down on the earth from outside creation as he monitors and controls the course of events, seems anachronistic and unreal to many Christians. Many understand God as being in the midst of us, actively working to redeem the world through the faith and faithfulness of those who pursue good for all their neighbors. The belief that everything that is to occur has already been decided in advance seems *fatalistic*.

In the context of *dispensationalist* thought, determinism frees the saved from moral accountability, assuming their justification and righteousness and de-emphasizing the importance of moral consistency. This tendency surfaces in the novels by Tim LaHaye and Jerry Jenkins, *The Left Behind Series*, where deception and violence become means to a justifiable end in the war between good and evil.[11] It suggests a proliferation of what Dietrich Bonhoeffer called "cheap grace."[12]

Biblical Literalism: While all Christians rely upon the Scriptures of the Old and New Testament as the primary standard for faith, many do not support *biblical literalism* or regard Scripture as infallible. Most see that not all Scripture is equally helpful, binding, or inspired. The diversity of perspectives on God and history represented by the biblical authors, as well as their divergent interpretations of faithfulness toward God and creation, reflects the dynamic interaction between the divine and the human. Mainstream Christians acknowledge the complex human factors in the interpretation of truth and the revelation of God among those first moved by God to compose the sacred texts and those inspired to study, interpret, teach, and preach them today. Many shrink from presuming that God can be defined in terms of any system of thought, whether rational or supra-rational. For the majority of mainline Christians, the authority of Scripture rests not in its divine authorship so much as in its power to convey a transforming experience of divine grace and to guide humanity toward whole and holy living, unto eternal life.

> Review your denomination's position on the authority and interpretation of Scripture. What authority do scriptural texts have in your life and why?

The carefully delineated *dispensationalist theory* depends on the accuracy and divine authority of *apocalyptic prophecy*. It requires, moreover, that biblical *apocalypses* be understood as not only infallible but, for the most part, yet to be fulfilled. This last assumption requires a leap of faith that seems difficult in light of the long history of events and theological experimentation since the close of the canon. Careful study of the texts indicates that some of the *prophecy* is actually after the fact (*ex eventu*). This does not invalidate the work but suggests that the worth of the material must be found in its pastoral intent, rather than in its power to accurately predict events that will occur two thousand years in the future. The likelihood, from the perspective of literary criticism and in light of historical analysis, is that the seers addressed their own times with a vital expectation that everything they predicted would occur very soon.

The disclosures made to these authors were in every instance received and interpreted, recorded and preserved by men who had particular concerns, biases, vocabularies, and historical contexts through which they interpreted highly subjective religious experiences. Moreover, all were deeply immersed in an *apocalyptic* school of thought, including a history of ideas, a literary genre, and a set of rhetorical practices that provided an established vernacular for communicating their beliefs. A thorough understanding of their work cannot be achieved apart from recognition of the origins of their thought and the needs that they and their audiences felt.

Dualism: Yet another tenet of *dispensationalist* thought that deserves scrutiny is its intrinsic *dualism*. Those who support the *doctrine of the rapture* assume that humanity can be divided into two camps, the righteous and the unrighteous or the saved and the lost. This tends to exonerate the believer and demonize the skeptic. *Dispensationalists* also assume that the originally good creation is now condemned. This negative evaluation of human history and the physical world absolves the believer of serving as a source of blessing to creation and an agent of reconciliation in the midst of conflict. It reduces the historical relevance of the gospel and strips it of its proclamation of social justice. It limits the work of *evangelism* to saving otherwise lost souls.

> * If *evangelism* is not only for the saving of souls, what is its purpose? Refer to Jesus' ministry of proclaiming the gospel, as you develop your own working definition and statement of purpose for *evangelism*.

Responsible Evangelism in Light of Jesus

The gospel that Jesus preached and demonstrated provided present help for the poor, the sick, the despised, and those excluded from salvation by the religious elite of his day. It relied on the power of every individual to choose and, thus, to change his or her future. Jesus dared to hope that the entire people of God could cooperate with God's purpose to redeem the world. He envisioned a blessed way of living and described its ethical implications, pronouncing those who lived God's way blessed in light of the reversal of conditions that was already beginning to take place. He relied

> **Closing**
> Read aloud the words to the hymn, "O Holy City Seen of John." Hum the tune in unison. Pause to pray extemporaneously for the coming of the kingdom of God. Sing the hymn. Pray the Lord's Prayer.
> Close by exchanging the blessing:
>
> *The peace of the Lord be with you.*
> *And also with you.*

on selected passages of Hebrew Scripture and challenged other texts and popular interpretations of end-time *prophecy* that his opponents preferred. His form of evangelism addressed social, political, and religious institutions and practices, as well as individual hearts and minds. His message urged reform and offered help and hope to those who most needed them. Authentic Christian *evangelism* requires as much today.

Notes

1. Cambridge, Mass.: Harvard University Press, 1992, page 75.
2. Boyer, page 88.
3. Timothy P. Weber, *Living In the Shadow of the Second Coming*, New York: Oxford University Press, 1979; page 21.
4. Coker, page 47; c.f., William Kelly, editor, *The Collected Writing of J. Nelson Darby,* Vol. 11, Lectures on the Second Coming of Christ, Kingston on Thames—Ell Hill Bible and Tract Society, 1962; page 233.
5. Weber, page 21.
6. Ibid., page 22.
7. Ibid., pages 21–22.
8. Coker, page 47.
9. Ibid.
10. Herbert W. Bateman IV, editor, *Three Central Issues In Contemporary Dispensationalism*; Grand Rapids, Michigan: Kregel Publications, 1999; page 43).
11. Wheaton, Illinois: Tyndale House Publisher, 1995, 1996.
12. *The Cost of Discipleship*, New York: The Macmillan Company; page 45.

For More Information

Consider the variety of learning styles and personality types reflected in worship preferences and denominational diversity, for example, liturgical churches versus Pentecostal churches. Which do you prefer and why? What bearing might this have on your approach to end-time teachings? Do you prefer a logical approach, an intuitive and mystical knowing, the joy of corporate praise, or the drama of a narrative?

Compare the *eschatology* of the hymn, "Blessed Assurance" with that of the hymn, "God of Grace and God of Glory." What relevant insights surface in this study?

How do different approaches and expressions enrich the life of the church? Recall instances when these same differences have led to conflict and alienation. How might different people with different learning styles and worship preferences be led to see beyond metaphors, symbols, doctrines, and prejudices? Devise an exercise for your group in which such an experiment in unity could be conducted.

Learn more about modern biblical studies by reading "Modern Approaches to Biblical Study," *The New Oxford Annotated Bible,* or some equally helpful summary of literary criticism, form criticism, and redaction criticism.

CHAPTER 8
END-TIME TEACHINGS

The Relevance of End-Time Teachings: Proclaiming the Kingdom of God Today

The most critical issues raised by this study include unity among those who seek to follow Jesus and carry on his ministry in the world today, clarity of mission particularly in the area of *evangelism*, and the political implications of

> **Focus**
> Beginning to reconstruct an approach to facing the future by faith

the gospel. Each of these concerns affects real people every day. Lack of resolution undermines the work of the church and the reputation of the gospel.

The Effect of Dispensationalism

Dispensationalist teaching has led to multiple divisions within the church and among evangelical Protestants in particular.[1] The heightened emphasis it places upon the study of *apocalyptic prophecy*, as if it were a detailed chart of the future, has led to diverse conclusions and applications, all held with the certainty that each is divinely inspired. With that certainty frequently comes the belief that one's eternal destiny depends upon acceptance of a particular interpretation.

Because of a generally pessimistic assessment of history, adherents tend to shrink from social justice work. They believe that while good works may improve the lot of a few, human initiative can do nothing to reverse what has been divinely predetermined or foreseen. *Dispensationalist* preachers and authors use evidence of the present

Gathering

Exchange the greeting from Romans 1:7b:

"Grace to you and peace from God our Father and the Lord Jesus Christ."

Share each other's joys and concerns. Pray for one another.

Then unite your voices in a prayer for the church:

O God of all times and places, we pray for your Church, which is set today amid the perplexities of a changing order, and face to face with new tasks. Baptize her afresh in the life-giving spirit of Jesus. Bestow upon her a great responsiveness to duty, a swifter compassion with suffering, and an utter loyalty to your will. Help her to proclaim boldly the coming of your kingdom. Put upon her lips the ancient gospel of her Lord. Fill her with the prophets' scorn of tyranny, and with a Christlike tenderness for the heavyladen and downtrodden. Bid her cease from seeking her own life, lest she lose it. Make her valiant to give up her life to humanity, that, like her crucified Lord, she may mount by the path of the cross to a higher glory; through the same Jesus Christ our Lord. Amen.

(Walter Rauschenbusch, *Prayers of the Social Awakening*, Pilgrim Press, 1909)

corruption of the world to indicate the imminence of the end, rather than to call the church to work for systemic change.

Political Activism and End-Time Teaching

End-time *prophets* often seem to seize the *doctrine of the rapture* as a key element of their theology and worldview because they find comprehending biblical material less daunting a task than making a difference in the midst of global crisis. Still, some leading evangelists have made significant attempts to politicize their impact, motivated by a vision of creating the reign of Christ on earth. Consider Pat Robertson and Jerry Falwell as examples. They look for a

* From your point of view, why is *evangelism* an urgent matter in the world today? Develop a consensus statement and consider a means of reporting and acting on your work. Covenant with one another to present your statement to an appropriate body within your church and to seek to implement your intentions.

day when the world will be governed by a theocracy. Among the many political issues that have rallied diverse groups of *dispensationalist* evangelicals have been the rise of Israel and the recovery of Jerusalem as the capital of the Jewish state. These groups see such events as heralding the soon coming reign of Christ whom they expect to rule from Jerusalem.

> What role has the *conservative evangelical* and fundamentalist support for the nation of Israel played in international politics, possibly including the rise of Arab terrorism and the ensuing American offensive against nations that sponsor it?

Concerns About Rapture Theology and Fundamentalism Today

When attempting to analyze and evaluate *dispensationalist* thought, and the *doctrine of the rapture* in particular, a number of serious concerns surface. The popular interest in the Final Judgment and the *apocalyptic* events that are to precede it mirrors increased tolerance and fascination with violence in the global community. The *dispensationalist* thought-world develops a program of cosmic vengeance, rather than of healing and forgiveness. With *fundamentalism* and *apocalyptic* fervor can come a willingness to sacrifice the foundations of moral behavior for the pursuit of perceived truth and justice as the believers define them. In many instances throughout history, the passion with which believers subscribed to this worldview led to armed violence and death. Rennie Schoepflin of LaSierra University concludes, "In a real sense an apocalyptic God is a divisive God, not an inclusive God. And just as this view of God has led Jews, Christians, and Muslims to see themselves as the elect and others as the damned, and to wage holy war on God's behalf, so the Apocalypse is the ultimate, final, holy war."[2]

When we demonize our enemies, we can justify hating them and wishing them destruction "in the hands of an angry God" (Jonathan Edwards, 1741). The recent resurgence of civil religion, as manifest during WWII, the Gulf War, and post-9/11, for example, demonstrates the power of labeling an adversary "evil" while praying or singing, "God Bless America." This spiritual culture implies that initiatives toward reconciliation among diverse or opposing people may be both irrelevant and unChristian. The theology behind much of what passes as evangelical Christianity despairs of any hope for historical peace in the world, as we

How is simply believing and accepting what you are told related to perceived powerlessness? How does religious education empower people?

How are family values related to sex-role stereotyping, and why do these find so much support among fundamentalists? Consider ultra-conservative Islamic, Jewish, and Christian fundamentalists in answering this question.

What evidence of fear do you see associated with the presence in your area of persons of various ethnic and religious backgrounds? How does such fear relate to end-time thinking among people you know?

now know it. It discourages acting upon the teachings and practice of Jesus as recorded in the Sermon on the Mount (Matthew 5–7).[3]

The *apocalyptic* culture reveals the powerlessness that its adherents feel. This sense of impotence may condition them to submit to authoritarian or charismatic leaders. The typical practices of excluding women from positions of power and sex-role stereotyping may be related to the broader sense of helplessness that underlies the theology of this movement. Another indicator of fear and dependency surfaces when these communities discourage liberal education and critical scholarship. Moreover, *dispensationalist* thought creates a spiritual elite among adherents. They are the "saved." This exclusivism parallels that of the Sadducees and Pharisees, a form of piety that Jesus resisted when he opposed the sabbath and purity laws of his day while eating and drinking with sinners.

Give examples from the history of the United States when political and religious leaders have identified an anti-Christ or have called a particular nation evil. Recall the emotion and the impact associated with those statements. Why are they dangerous uses of *apocalyptic* language?

---

* Why do many adults who think abstractly in dealing with social, political, and philosophical matters often use concrete, literal thinking in reading the Bible? How do you respond to the statement that the sign-seeking of *dispensationalist apocalyptic* "relies . . . on a concrete and literal interpretation of *apocalyptic literature,* which is more properly treated as sacred *myth*"? Look at the definition of *myth* in the Glossary. How can sacred *myths* be a vehicle of truth?

The sign-seeking that is so endemic to dispensationalist prophecy and teaching suggests an unhealthy fascination with that which, according to Jesus, cannot be known except by God. It indicates a misdirection of faith. It relies, moreover, on a concrete and literal interpretation of *apocalyptic literature*, which is more properly treated as sacred *myth*.

The Relevance of End-Time Teachings

Although ancient *apocalyptic literature* may or may not serve the work of God in the world today, its popularity reflects its timelessness. Something of its genre is clearly wanted and needed in modern *eschatology* because it addresses perennial and universal spiritual needs. The dramatic narrative style of *apocalyptic literature* makes it vastly more satisfying to the religious imagination than doctrinal statements or logical teaching.

Life feels flat and uninteresting to many North Americans raised on videogames and cinematography or satiated with material things and instant gratification. The recent rise in the popularity of the occult, psychic phenomena, astrology, mystery cults, and science fiction parallels the increased demand for end-time teachings derived from *apocalyptic* sources. The appetite for *apocalyptic* novels, films, preaching, and piety is not limited to the less educated or to a certain subculture. It has had an impact on a broad spectrum of society, involving people of all ages and backgrounds in a mediated drama, giving meaning to an otherwise chaotic clash of wills, weapons, words, and cultures.

Apocalyptic thinking invites a shift in perspective, an altered state of awareness, and access to the supernatural and eternal. When people change their perception of reality, a kind of conversion takes place. However, the question that must be asked and answered remains: Is the change that is taking place under the influence of rapturism and *apocalyptic* futurism in harmony with the vision of Jesus for the redemption of the world?

The Reliability of Jesus' Eschatology

Anyone looking back on the events of the first century, in light of Jesus' *eschatological* message and his expectation of the imminent consummation of history, has to ask the question, "Was Jesus a false *prophet*?" After all, the end of history did not come within the generation to which he addressed himself. Instead, the history of Israel as a nation with its own

> * Read Matthew 7:15-20 and Mark 13:14-23. Both passages refer to false *prophets*. One passage is clearly *apocalyptic* in its style and content. Note the differences and similarities between the false *prophets* under consideration. Determine what kind of *prophet* Jesus was. Did he primarily predict the future or proclaim the word of God? Develop your own rule for distinguishing between true and false *prophecy*, given your conclusion about the nature of Jesus' work. What makes a *prophet* true or false?

homeland came to a close. This tragedy, effected by the Roman invasion of Jerusalem in A.D. 70, dramatically influenced the development of Judaism and Christianity; but it did not achieve the ultimate defeat of evil and the triumph of righteousness. In terms of the traditional Jewish test of legitimate *prophecy*, which required that a *prophet's* predictions be proven by historical events, people might think of Jesus as a "false *prophet*."

Robert Jewett, a contemporary student of *apocalyptic* thought, proposes an alternative evaluation. He suggests that Jesus' real concern in preaching about imminent judgment was not the cosmic event that *apocalyptic prophets* supposed; but, rather, to warn that the "threatened city of Jerusalem and its 'children' who were bound for the dump heap of Gehenna, the smoldering image of the wrath that strikes down the illusions of nations or groups that fancy themselves safely on the side of angels," was at hand.[4] According to Jewett and others who evaluate Jesus' unfulfilled *prophecies* from a sympathetic point of view, Jesus used *apocalyptic* language to make the same kind of point that the great *prophets* before him had been making when they used *apocalyptic* imagery to warn of catastrophe ahead.

While Jesus anticipated the destruction of Jerusalem and dreaded it intensely, he prayed and worked for transformation at both personal and societal levels. Jesus frequently used hyperbole as a form of rhetoric, as did other rabbis of the period. He used *apocalyptic* categories in order to emphasize the urgency of his call to repentance and faith in divine redemption. Jesus wanted to counter the zealotry of violent revolutionaries and to awaken the consciences of the religious authorities. These authorities tolerated or profited from the same moral and religious corruption that had led to destruction and exile for earlier generations of Jews. Faithful Christian *eschatology* will do the work that Jesus did, the work of transformation of persons and of society.

Modernism and the Message of the Church Today

The modernism that the descendants of Charles Hodge and the *Dispensationalists* joined ranks to combat, continues to affect religious thought today. Reporting on what he called twentieth-century "moderns," Rennie Schoepflin said they "generally viewed prophetic time lines as quaint fossils of a bygone age. . . .Time moved according to no inherent purpose and with no end in sight that might give ultimate meaning for the present. . . . For moderns who still believed that God acted in history, he acted within nature in immanent, pantheistic ways or by way of the natural laws of the universe. . . . If there would be an end to history, it would come about as a result of the natural order of things or through the willful act of humans, not through the special providence of a transcendent God. In an ironic way, the law of extinction, by which the fit survive and the unfit die off, exerted its daily 'apocalypse' on the natural world. Whatever died, whatever system ceased to operate, endured its own personal apocalypse, an 'apocalypse' that was repeated time and again into an unseeable future."[5]

> Read and reread Rennie Schoepflin's description of the modern view of *apocalyptic*. Do you identify with any aspects of the modern point of view? If so, how? Do you agree or disagree with the statement, "the majority of the audience that the church addresses day in and day out no longer thinks in pre-scientific terms"? Explain your response. In light of this statement and your reflections on it, what approach should be taken to the work of *evangelism?*

While scientific rationalism no longer dominates spirituality in the twenty-first century, its authority persists as a corrective and guardian of mainstream theology. Biblical criticism continues to offer refreshing and challenging insights in the effort to take Scripture seriously and apply it meaningfully in a new era. Meanwhile, the majority of the audience that the church addresses day in and day out no longer thinks in pre-scientific terms.

Thinking and Speaking From Outside the Apocalyptic Worldview

The legitimate pastoral agenda behind end-time teaching lies in its critique of the dominant value structure and its concurrent offer of a viable alternative. The *apocalyptic* narrative approach successfully appeals to a variety of learning styles and personality types. Its vivid language engages the senses and the imagination. Its intricacy and symbolism challenge the intellect. Its passion appeals to the emotions and faith of believers. Its ecstatic hymns and glorious, mystical visions invite spiritual fulfillment. Any useful *eschatology* must do the same. Inasmuch as Jesus was an *eschatological prophet* who announced the imminent reign of God on earth and called for radical personal and cultural conversion, Christian theology and practice must continue to operate out of an *eschatological* creativity, even if it abandons the *apocalyptic worldview* and vernacular.

* What answer do you give to the question, Do you have faith in a transcendent power who guides all things? Why do you believe or not believe that "history [is] moving toward a blessed consummation"? How is the kingdom of God breaking into your world?

Karl Barth and Rudolph Bultmann de-historicized *eschatology* by giving it either a spiritual interpretation or proclaiming it wholly realized. The majority of twentieth-century theologians, however, maintained the future dimension of *eschatology*, but preferred to develop their thought from the beginning of time in God. Jürgen Moltmann, in his seminal work, *The Theology of Hope*, in referring to systematic theology, proclaimed that "eschatology should not be its end, but its beginning."[6]

Thomas Finger, a theologian of the Believers' Church tradition within which Mennonites and the Church of the Brethren are prominent members, says that the problem of evil will, in the twenty-first century, be the greatest obstacle to faith in God; and that, therefore, providing a theology of last things that upholds the belief that good will ultimately triumph over evil will be critical to encouraging the saints and to evangelical work.[7] Responsible end-time teachings, regardless of their genre and vocabulary, must deal both with things feared and things hoped for, as well as with the dread and the hope that these expected events arouse in believers. Constructive initiatives in dealing with complex socio/political, ecological, and scientific issues will follow out of a viable *eschatology*. It is time to exorcise the demons of our times with the moral authority and spiritual grace of divine Goodness.

A useful *eschatology* will respond with appropriate humility and reserve to critical twenty-first–century religious questions: Who's in charge of our world? How can we orient ourselves in the midst of chaos? When and how will good triumph over evil? How is God exercising authority in the world today? Do we have faith in a transcendent power who guides all things? Is history moving toward a blessed consummation? If we propose to answer in a constructive manner, we must think from the future redemption toward the present crisis. Theology must dare to speak and act in light of the in-breaking kingdom of God.

> Which of the following questions seems most important to you: Who's in charge of our world? How can we orient ourselves in the midst of chaos? When and how will good triumph over evil? How is God exercising authority in the world today? How would you respond if someone you know asked one of these questions?

The historic doctrines of the *second coming of Christ,* hell, and the ultimate redemption of creation, including life after life and bodily resurrection, remain elements of the creeds that unite mainstream Christian churches. They lack currency, however, in the faith of many modern and postmodern practitioners. They must be studied again, but not as literal promises to be fulfilled at some future date. Rather, they need to be prized as ancient icons by which God's people have approached mystery and been illuminated or corrected in every generation.

Conclusions

What a grave disservice we do to a great work of art when we examine it as if with a magnifying glass, rather than beholding it at a distance in its entirety. When in awe we stand before or sit in the moment of an inspired work, we participate in it. We are shaped by it. We breathe its majesty. We partake of its creative power. It is with this measure of reverence that postmodern seekers and faithful believers must approach again the doctrines of our tradition that point to the as-yet-unfulfilled dimensions of God's reign. Then, and only then, will we surrender ourselves to the hope that good will triumph; having determined in advance that, regardless of what the future holds, we will love and serve the good alone.

Eschatology is clearly vital to an authentically biblical and responsible Christian theology and practice. People everywhere desperately need to recover a transcendent vision. The ability to see beyond what is apparent can set us free from self-interested behavior patterns. It can liberate us to

Read Mark 1:14-15. Recall images of Jesus' ministry. Compare and contrast the account of Jesus' ministry with that of John the Baptist in Matthew 3:1-10. Reconsider the statement, "Lasting conversion comes by way of the winsome power of grace, rather than by the insidious power of fear." How did the ministry of Jesus illustrate the truth of this principle?

courageously engage in the work of global citizenship.

We live on the edge of history, ready to break through the horizon. The future can be God's reign among us. Any good *eschatology* will address the need to recover divinely inspired hope, passion, and love.

The moral and spiritual authority of any *eschatology* rests in its power to redeem both individuals and multiple generations of believers, as well as entire communities. For this reason, we direct our attention again to Jesus and acknowledge his authority, grace, and power to redeem us and our world in these dangerous times. Because through him we see all that is best—all that creates, sustains, and redeems life—we follow him. Lasting conversion comes by way of the winsome power of grace rather than by the insidious power of fear.

The teachings of Jesus provide the vision of goodness rising above all that demeans and destroys life. At the crux of the Christian hope, being worked out every day around the globe, is the possibility and potential for repentance and faith met by the transforming goodness we call God. The divine mercy seat, the place of atonement, appears everywhere that the character of Christ is revealed through authentic witness.[8] Out of conversion emerges an energetic commitment to address the real world with its potential for thermonuclear disaster and its epidemic of moral failure and global hatred. Twenty-first–century students of Jesus must work at applying his message to contemporary issues, much as the skill and imagination of the artist and her paints bring a pencil drawing to life on canvas or as an inspired composer takes notes and makes music of them.

The spirit of goodness, a transcendent creative and redemptive power, is at work among us. What Jesus announced in first-century Palestine remains equally true today. Whenever and wherever people live in love toward one another, God is present and incarnate. Our art, music, dance, worship, writing, *prophecy*, and witness in formal and informal settings can declare the vibrant vitality of divine power at work in the midst of suffering, dying, sin, repentance, and reconciliation.

Because we long to live in a just universe, we work for justice in our own localities. Because we recognize the source of life and goodness as being both beyond ourselves and among us, we practice ways of connecting and reconnecting with God, so that life can flow through us to others more freely and more consistently. In these ways, we daily restore the foundations of hope.

> * Give examples of people you know who are taking their faith to the real-life issues of the twenty-first–century world. What is your response to the statement that faithful people generally long for "universal peace and communion with God"? Pray that you and they will find fresh ways to hope and work together toward these ends.

The destructive forces that inspire division, elitism, and violence will continue to wreak havoc. Those who resist must exercise vigorous diligence to keep their devotion and focus clear. Faithful people long for the realization of universal peace and communion with God. Though the end of the struggle may not be within sight, the way to the end remains clear. The long-trod path of devotional practice, corporate worship, faithful work, and constant witness remains the reliable road today.

In the meantime, as we live and work beside fundamentalist believers for whom *apocalyptic* thinking remains an important motivator, we can do so with enhanced appreciation for their concerns and their faith. Their witness can serve as a clarion call to take evil seriously and to remain spiritually alert. We can demonstrate gracious, reconciling love toward them with the hope of earning from them some sense of positive neighborly regard, if not warm inclusion among the elect. We can remember with them the apostle Paul's words, "Do not be overcome by evil, but overcome evil with good" (Romans 12:21).

> **Closing**
> Read Romans 12:14-21. Pray silently for one another and for worldwide peace.
>
> Pray the Lord's Prayer.
> Exchange signs of peace and the blessing
> *The peace of the Lord be with you.*
> *And also with you.*

Notes

1. Weber, pages 181–82.

2. "Apocalypse in an Age of Science," in *The Encyclopedia of Apocalypticism, Vol. 3* edited by Stephen J. Stein; New York: Continuum, 1998; page 429.

3. William Vance Trollinger, Jr., "How John Nelson Darby Went Visiting," in *Apocalypticism and Millennialism*, Loren L. Johns, editor; Kitchener, Ontario: Pandora Press, 2000; page 279.

4. Robert Jewett, *Jesus Against the Rapture: Seven Unexpected Prophecies;* Philadelphia: Westminster Press, 1979; pages 90–91.

5. "Apocalypse in an Age of Science," page 436.

6. New York: Harper and Row, 1967, page 16.

7. "Outlines of a Contemporary Believers Church Eschatology" in *Apocalypticism and Millennialism*; page 296.

8. Romans 3:25; see alternative translation notes, *Oxford Annotated New Revised Standard Version*.

APPENDIX

Glossary

amillennial(ism; ist): the school of thought that expects no literal reign of Christ on earth; one who holds to this belief.

Ancient of Days: name designating the judge in Daniel 7:9 in the King James Version. Scholars differ on whether it refers to God or to the Angel of God.

Ancient One: New Revised Standard Version translation of the name in Daniel 7:9; same as "Ancient of Days"

apocalypse: revelation or the unveiling of a divine secret

apocalyptic(ism): that which is disclosed or revealed; refers to grotesque, extreme, end-time images that frequently occur in visions

apocalyptic eschatology: thought regarding the end of history from the perspective of revelation received through a visionary experience, as interpreted by an apocalyptic prophet, that indicates that history is about to end

apocalyptic literature: written prophecy regarding the close of history, based on a narrative including crisis, judgment, and salvation, which is found in Iranian, Egyptian, Greek, Jewish and Christian cultures of the *classical period*

apocalyptic prophet/prophecy: a seer who has been guided into the heavenly realm and given otherwise unavailable foresight regarding that which is yet to occur at the close of history or regarding the heavenly domain itself; the content of that foresight

apocalyptic worldview: a linear view of history that is based in the belief that a sovereign God initiated, guides, intervenes, and will consummate the course of events in a predetermined manner, as disclosed through visions and interpreted to divinely inspired prophets

apokastasis: Greek for the end-time transformation of the earth either into a restored paradise or a new creation

beatific vision: a mystical experience in which one sees either God or Christ

biblical inerrancy: the doctrine that all Scripture is God's teaching and is without mistakes or contradictions

biblical literalism: the practice of taking the words and images of the Bible in their most basic sense without regard for exaggeration, historical bias, or metaphorical interpretation, based on the treatment of the words of Scripture as intrinsically sacred and not subject to interpretation or evaluation

conservative evangelical: describes Protestant Christians who subscribe to the tenets of *fundamentalism*

day of the Lord: the consummation of history when a heavenly figure will come to judge all people, defeat Satan and his allies, banish them to hell, and restore paradise

Dead Sea Scrolls: writings of an Essene community; discovered in 1947 by the Dead Sea

diaspora: the dispersion of the Jews outside of their homeland to surrounding countries of exile and refuge

dispensationalist(m): a system of beliefs or adherents thereof that divides history into eras or ages, based on a literal interpretation of Revelation and Daniel

doctrine of the rapture: see *rapture, doctrine of the*

dualism: a division of the world, its people, or individuals into two independent states or pcinciples; the religious doctrine that the universe contains opposed forces of good and evil, seen as relatively balanced equals as in Zoroastrianism

early church fathers: the leaders of the Christian church up to around A.D. 600

eschatological vision: an active anticipation of the close of history

eschatology/eschatological: the study of last things, derived from the Greek word *eschatos*, which means "last"

eschaton: the close of the age; the end of time

Essenes: a Jewish separatist community with quarters in Jerusalem, Galilee, and the Judean Wilderness at Qumran, dating from c. 130 B.C. to A.D. 68

evangelism: preaching or bearing witness to the gospel or good news, from the Greek *evangelion*

ex eventu: see *prophecy ex eventu*

fatalism: the belief that all events are determined in advance and inevitable

fundamentalism: a belief system and movement that is generally considered ultra-conservative. Within Protestant Christianity, the publication between 1910 and 1915 of a set of tracts called *The Fundamentals* defended the literal interpretation and inerrancy of Scripture, as well as orthodox doctrine.

general resurrection: the apocalyptic belief that the dead will rise from their graves for the Last Judgment at the last day

Gnosticism/Gnostic: religious movements in the first century that offered salvation from the oppressive bonds of material existence through knowledge; seen as heresy by early Christians; a person who followed such a movement.

hermeneutic: theory of interpretation

hyperbolic: of or related to hyperbole; a deliberately exaggerated statement not meant to be taken literally

intertestamental period: between approximately 300 B.C. and A.D. 50

mainstream scholars: experts in biblical studies outside of the *conservative evangelical* and *dispensationalist* schools of thought

millennium, millennialism(t), millennial reign: one thousand years of peace under the authority of Christ before the ultimate defeat of Satan and the Final Judgment (a belief held and debated in the Patristic Period and known as Chiliasm); one who holds this belief

myth/mythology: a traditional narrative, such as parable, allegory, folklore, legend, or fable, usually involving supernatural or imaginary persons and embodying popular ideas on natural or social phenomena or addressing ultimate concerns

mythic: that which is of or pertains to the literary genre of mythology

Parousia: the Greek word for "coming," refers to the advent of the Messiah, the coming of the Son of Man on the clouds of heaven at the close of history, or the second coming of Christ.

postexilic: after the exile of the Hebrew people to Babylon, beginning in 539 B.C. with their return to their homeland

postmillennial(ism; ist): the school of thought that anticipates the Second Coming to follow the present reign of Christ on earth; one who holds this belief

premillennial(ism; ist): the belief that the second coming of Christ will occur before Christ inaugurates his thousand-year reign on earth; one who holds this belief.

prophecy: predictions about the future or forth-telling the Word of God to inspire, convert, warn, or condemn.

prophecy ex eventu (after the fact): a pseudonymous proclamation, purportedly given by a seer who lived long before the actual writing of the prophecy, regarding events that have already occurred at the time of publication but that had not yet occurred within the lifetime of the supposed prophet. The author's purpose in publishing such fictitious predictions is to validate the medium of prophecy and to borrow authority from an earlier and established prophet.

prophet: any inspired individual who believes that he has been sent by his god with a message to tell others; one who speaks for God

pseudonym: an assumed name, rather than the name by which the author is normally known

Q or Quelle (Source): represents a German scholarly hypothesis regarding a common collection of the sayings of Jesus used by Matthew and Luke, but not available to Mark

rapture, doctrine of the: teaching that the Lord will come for his saints, both living and dead, before the tribulation and will take them to be with him in safety

The Revelation to John: a detailed title for Revelation that includes the self-ascribed name of the author

second coming of Christ: phrase that refers to the future return or "parousia" of Christ

shamans: native seers and healers, the spiritual guides of primitive religions who often use(d) magic to control events, cure the sick, or divine the hidden

Son of Man: a heavenly judge who will be given dominion over the earth at the close of history, originally derived from Daniel 7:13-14. Jesus may have used the term to refer to himself as a man as in "Son of Man." He may also have used the term to refer to the coming end of the age. The

Synoptic Gospels present him as identifying himself with the figure from Daniel 7. In Daniel 7:13, the Aramaic words *bar enash* are translated as "son of man" in the King James and New International Versions of the Bible and as "a human being" in the New Revised Standard Version.

sovereign: ultimate authority or supreme ruler

Sybilline Oracles: predictions of the future, made by the female prophet Sybil and her disciples, which were widely circulated throughout the Mediterranean basin in the first century A.D.

syncretism: the blending of foreign religious ideas with older Jewish beliefs and practices

Synoptic Gospels: Matthew, Mark, and Luke. Scholarly study has revealed material common to all three Gospels, material in Matthew and Luke that are not in Mark, and material peculiar to each Gospel.

theological determinism: philosophy of history and a system of thinking about God that teaches that historical events are predetermined according to "the definite plan and foreknowledge of God" (Acts 2:23)

tribulation: refers to a long period of suffering and cosmic disaster during the end times

universal history: refers to the concept of a series of events encompassing all of creation; a contribution made by apocalypticism to the history of ideas

YHWH: Tetragrammaton, a Greek word that means "having four letters," representing the name of God that was not to be pronounced

APPENDIX

An Overview of the Twelve Tribes

The Twelve Tribes is a communal movement of approximately 2,500 men, women, and children in sixteen locations within the U.S. and eight locations outside the U.S. They live out of an apocalyptic vision, based on a literal interpretation of the Bible and the motivation to become the twelve tribes of the true Israel who will reign with Christ during the Millennium. While they are premillennialists, they are not dispensationalists. They expect to endure persecution and trouble, rather than escape them through what some anticipate as the rapture of the church. They have already experienced a great deal of resistance, invasion, violent attacks, and false accusations. They anticipate Christ's return in approximately fifty years, after at least one more generation of members has grown to young adulthood within the purity of the community. It is these holy ones whom they expect to be fit to judge the nations.

The Twelve Tribes is a separatist and evangelistic movement that hopes to provide a haven for those who feel lost or alienated from Christianity and the sinful world at large. Hospitality is a key feature of their approach to the public. They own and operate several cafés that are open to the public and serve healthy foods and beverages. In their practice of welcoming strangers and offering them food and shelter, they also offer their *Freepaper*, which describes their purpose, origin, and foundational beliefs.

They believe, among other things, that Messiah will come when twelve tribes have finally been established. They work to build those tribes of holy people in several ways. First, they have renounced sinful ways, private property, and the right to self-determination, so as to seek God's will in every aspect of their lives. They attempt to practice the lifestyle of the early church at Jerusalem, as described in Acts 2 and 3, and believe that they cannot obey Christ without selling all they have and "laying it at the apostles' feet" (Acts 4:37). They conduct a wide range of cottage industries to support their communities. These industries include a number of crafts and trades to which teenaged members can be apprenticed, according to their interest and ability.

Children attend a structured home-schooling program in each community for four days a week. On the fifth day, the children of school age work beside a parent or other adult mentor. Youth engage in a more extensive apprenticeship until they have completed their mandatory formal education and are ready to join the community's work force. Higher education is not provided. Some members have, however, entered the Twelve Tribes after having gained university and graduate-level training. Members largely limit their reading to the Bible and the *Freepaper*. The community does not expose itself to radio, television, or movies. Children do not own manufactured toys. The music that they enjoy is Jewish folk music adapted for worship and religious celebration, which includes folk dancing. Their membership includes a number of skilled illustrators and fine artists.

Before and after work or school each day, the community gathers within each residence for a half hour of corporate prayer, confession, exhortation, and teaching. Meals are taken together in the residence, which may house several family units and single adults. A typical nuclear family will use two rooms within a large house. A common living and eating area is customary. Women and girls wear long hair, loosely fitting pantaloons and blouses or modest, long dresses, practical shoes, and a head scarf. Men and boys wear simple work clothes, practical shoes, beards, and long hair bound in a string. Men and boys can be found wearing head bands, preparing themselves to wear the heavenly royal diadem. They eat organically grown foods and avoid caffeine and alcoholic beverages, except for wine in their equivalent of Holy Communion on the sabbath. Members enjoy their mealtimes as occasions for refreshment, celebration, and community life. Friday is used for work and for both physical and spiritual preparation for the sabbath, which begins with a gathering time and festive meal on Friday evening after sunset. Sunday, or First Day, is a day of community work projects and family recreation.

The highly supportive communal lifestyle, based on conservative and nonmaterialistic values, creates a relaxed and apparently healthy atmosphere for the mostly young members. Women fulfill traditional responsibilities including raising children, preparing meals, providing clothing, managing the communal households, and working within various handcraft industries. A few older adults live in the communities and continue productive lives. Men provide for the community through their trades.

All men are strongly encouraged to marry and bear sons, with the goal that they will become the generation of pure and holy ones who will reign with Christ. Children are raised under the constant supervision of the community and are provided clear boundaries, including corporal punishment as needed. Discipline is closely defined and monitored by the community. Instruction in family life is a common element of the exhortation and oversight that is given in communal gatherings.

Members often receive new Hebrew names after their character has been identified and developed. The mother is called by the Hebrew word for "Foundation" and the father is similarly called "Source." Members believe that only the holy who have left the world, have surrendered all rights to personal property, and have given themselves entirely to following Yeshua (Hebrew for Jesus) have received the Holy Spirit. For this reason, they reserve the Hebrew greeting, "Shalom," for one another.

They consider themselves messianic and the true Israelites. They believe themselves to be the first people who have been faithful to the will of God. Thus, they believe that their movement will provide the 144,000 to be sealed against eternal destruction during the tribulation. They expect that the mission of the Twelve Tribes shall be to proclaim the gospel to the nations during the tribulation and that they will be martyred for so doing. The Twelve Tribes predict that the institutional churches will fail or be destroyed because of internal corruption and misrepresentation of the gospel

The Twelve Tribes acknowledge, however, that not all people who live outside their communal movement are filthy and bound for hell at the Day of Judgment. They recognize that many live according to a clear conscience and consistently choose to live in love toward their neighbors. These are the righteous. While the holy will rule them, they will enjoy the blessings of the Millennial Reign. If they die before Messiah comes, however, their souls will await the general resurrection and endure the consequences of their guilt, inasmuch as they will not have lived pure and holy lives.

(This information was gleaned from several interviews with members of the Twelve Tribes, *Freepapers*, and the Twelve Tribes Web site.)

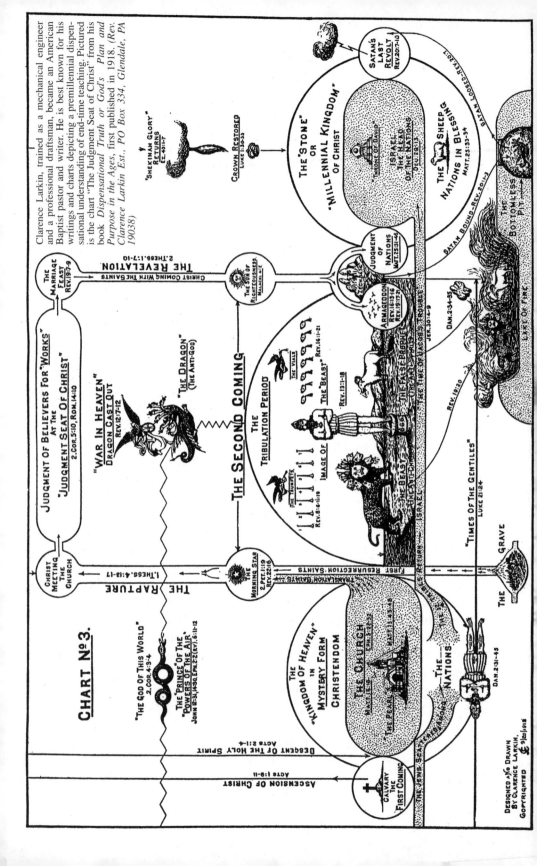

CHART N° 3.

Clarence Larkin, trained as a mechanical engineer and a professional draftsman, became an American Baptist pastor and writer. He is best known for his writings and charts depicting a premillennial dispensational understanding of end-time teaching. Pictured is the chart "The Judgment Seat of Christ" from his book *Dispensational Truth or God's Plan and Purpose in the Ages*, first published in 1918. (Rev. Clarence Larkin Est., PO Box 334, Glendale, PA 19038)

JUDGMENT OF BELIEVERS FOR "WORKS" At The "JUDGMENT SEAT OF CHRIST" 2.COR.5:10. ROM.14:10

"WAR IN HEAVEN" DRAGON CAST OUT Rev.12:7-12

"THE DRAGON" (The Anti-God)

THE MARRIAGE FEAST REV.19:7-9

THE REVELATION 2.THESS.1:7-10

CHRIST COMING WITH THE SAINTS

THE SON OF RIGHTEOUSNESS MALACHI 4:2

"SHEKINAH GLORY" RETURNS EZ.43:1-7

CROWN RESTORED LUKE 1:30-33

THE "STONE" OR "MILLENNIAL KINGDOM" OF CHRIST

SATAN'S LAST REVOLT Rev.20:7-10

"THRONE OF DAVID"

ISRAEL THE HEAD OF THE NATIONS DEU.28:13

THE SHEEP NATIONS IN BLESSING MAT.25:33-34

SATAN BOUND-REV.20:1-3

SATAN LOOSED-REV.20:7

THE SECOND COMING

THE TRIBULATION PERIOD

THE VIALS Rev.16:1-21

"THE BEAST" Rev.13:1-18

IMAGE OF THE BEAST Rev.13:14-15

666 THE BEAST (The Anti-Christ)

THE FALSE PROPHET Or The Lamb-like Beast

JUDGMENT OF NATIONS MAT.25:31-46

ARMAGEDDON Rev.16:13-16 Rev.19:17-21

THE TRUMPET Rev.8:6-11:19

THE WARS Rev.6:1-8:1

DAN.2:34-35

"THE TIME OF JACOB'S TROUBLE" JER.30:4-9

CHRIST MEETING THE CHURCH

THE RAPTURE

1.THESS. 4:13-17

THE MORNING STAR 2.PET.1:19 REV.22:16

TRANSLATION SAINTS

FIRST RESURRECTION SAINTS

RETURN OF ISRAEL

"TIMES OF THE GENTILES" LUKE 21:24

REV.18:20

THE BOTTOMLESS PIT

THE GRAVE

LAKE OF FIRE

"THE GOD OF THIS WORLD" 2.COR.4:3-4

THE "PRINCE OF THE "POWERS OF THE AIR". JOHN 12:31,14:30.EPH.2:2(RV).6:11-12

DESCENT OF THE HOLY SPIRIT ACTS 2:1-4

ASCENSION OF CHRIST ACTS 1:9-11

THE "KINGDOM OF HEAVEN" IN MYSTERY FORM CHRISTENDOM

THE CHURCH MAT.16:18 EPH.3:1-12 MAT.13:33-52

THE NATIONS

DAN.2:31-45

THE JEWS SCATTERED AMONG THE NATIONS

CALVARY THE FIRST COMING

DESIGNED AND DRAWN BY CLARENCE LARKIN. COPYRIGHTED